Bartender as a Business

By Jason Littrell

Absolute Author
Publishing House

Publisher: Absolute Author Publishing House
Editor: Jan Littrell
Interior Designer: Dr. Melissa Caudle
Cover Designer: Rebeca @RebecaCovers

ISBN: 978-1-64953-039-4

1. Bartending 2. Occupation   3. Business

For Jasper.

TABLE OF CONTENTS

Introduction

What is the difference between a bartender and a business? Aside from the steady gig, there isn't much. We work long hours, we sell things to people, we're creative, and if we don't work, we don't eat.

So what's the difference?

As a business owner, your job is to build a BRAND and a SYSTEM so that someday, you won't have to work anymore, but you still earn money.

It doesn't matter the economy, the weather, the political climate, or even if there's a global pandemic. You can create value for individuals and other businesses, whether IN or OUTSIDE of the hospitality industry. Chances are you already do; you just haven't structured it that way.

This book goes through exactly how to do that, and to put you on the path of self-determination. By this, I mean leveraging the unique skills and experiences you have to build a company that provides incredible insight and value for its customers.

Let's get your business started.

Jason Littrell
September 2020

Jason Littrell

PART ONE: MINDSET

Chapter 1

Becoming a Brand

If you don't work, you don't eat. What is the difference between you and a business owner?

I wrote this for the professional mixologist or bartender or chef who wants to break through the limitations of shift work and grow a career as an independent industry professional. You're already an entrepreneur, so why not take things one step further? Re-orient your thinking about your role. Shift your self-concept from shift worker to an independent business owner. You are the safest investment you will ever make.

2

In this book, I will encourage you to look at your career in a new way. You will learn some straightforward techniques and ideas that you can use to build a long-term career as an independent food and beverage professional. Do you want a retirement plan or paid vacations? No problem, just build them into your business plan. Your business is YOU.

What is the difference between an entrepreneur and a shift worker? Both devote their skill sets to the establishment, and both are involved in creating consumer experiences that require creativity, imagination, a great deal of skill, long hours, and a high tolerance for workplace bullshit. What if you were to take the skills, expertise, experience, and personal attributes that you have developed all these years and funneled them all into your own business? If you did that, the possibilities for you extend far beyond the whims of one employer.

I used to be like you. I was a bartender who loved his job working at one of the best bars in the world. I was having a great time meeting incredible people. Everything was going great. But I had no savings, no credit, and no idea what would happen next, and I knew I was only one broken bone away from being unemployed.

And then I broke my arm.

You might be as vulnerable as I was. You don't have a clear vision of how to build your career, or what should or might happen beyond your current job. All of your income is dependent on your labor, not your knowledge. It's about your remarkable ability to mix those margaritas and marinate that carp right that ensures you're getting an income. The idea of having a sustainable income based on what you **know** rather than what you **do** seems beyond your reach. But it doesn't have to be.

This book will provide actionable advice on steps you can take to get off the hamster wheel and control your career on your terms. You will learn how to negotiate and plan for a better future that doesn't depend on anyone but yourself and your support network. You deserve it.

What is Your Brand?

Bartending is a truly honorable profession. I believe this with all my heart, and the purpose of this book is not to denigrate shift work. I love the job, and I assume you do too. When you are just another person behind the curtain whose money is earned at the expense of your youth and your body, that's a problem.

The drinks you make is making others happy, but what about your happiness?

4

The difference is becoming a brand. Your brand will distinguish you from all the other bartenders and will provide you with some security. As you grow, your brand grows with you and becomes a crucial element in your growth. Your brand is what you have to offer to the marketplace, beyond your ability to make duck a l'orange. Many people have the same skills as you, but nobody has the same brand.

Your brand is your big ideas, your reputation, your personality, your unique combination of knowledge and experience. Selling your brand (rather than merely your skillset) opens you up to a whole new world of buyers who depend on people like you for solutions.

You are the Brand, Now Make it a Business

No matter how much you like your job or what your goals are, when you start a job, you are interviewing. Why? Because tending bar requires knowing how to do a set of tasks, a knowledge that a lot of people have. When a job posting says, "experience required," it is assumed that you have mastery of specific tasks to be considered for the job. But beyond tasks, your job also requires creativity, hard work, personal connections, and repetitive physical and mental stress. While it can be fun sometimes, it isn't fun all the time. But even work that can be fun and personally gratifying also comes with long-term uncertainties.

Pamela Wiznitzer is an excellent example of how to transition from bartender to business. Her start was not unlike my own; she was your typical bartender who worked at a bar in Murray Hill in New York City. In 2009, she read an issue of Time Out New York about star bartenders in the city. That was when she realized that her job could be much more than shift work. She decided to pursue bartending as a business.

Today, Pam is one of the most sought-after brands in the industry due to her engagement with the industry, consumers, and social media savvy. She has branched out far beyond tending bar and has become a lifestyle and media influencer.

Bartenders love to get together to drink and talk. For some, running a bar alone is enough, but for others, it isn't. Some bartenders say the "bubble has burst" and that a well-made cocktail is no longer the exception. It's now the rule. Media trends (social and mass) are driving global change at a breath-taking speed.

Where will you be in five years? The risk you take starting a business is not unlike the risk you are taking every day as an at-will employee. If you have the ambition and desire to secure a financial future for yourself and your family, create your own business. The only alternative is the one in front of you right now--a job that promises you nothing and takes everything.

It is a common misconception that you have to risk your current job to start a business. You don't. You can stay in your career while you create your business. It's encouraged and is the only practical route for most people. You can do both while continuing to learn on the job.

Starting a Business: The Absolute Basics

Starting a business is not as difficult as you might think. Yes, there is some paperwork and expense involved, but nothing that you could consider insurmountable. Don't even think about "winging it" without formally and officially starting your own business. Start this process today. I encourage you to bill for your time to learn or knowledge brokering.

Step 1: Register your business with your state. While strictly speaking this isn't completely necessary, it's recommended. It's typically a simple process; just Google "business start-up [your state]" and you will likely come across a resource that gives you step-by-step instructions and forms for your state.

You will need to decide what type of business you are. The choices are sole proprietorship, general partnership, limited liability partnership (LLP), or S-Corporation. If you want to keep it simple for now, knowing you can always change it later, define yourself as a sole proprietor. A general partnership is when two or more people form an alliance and agree to do business together. A limited liability partnership (LLP) is a special kind of general company, which provides the simplicity and flexibility of an organization without the unlimited liability.

Another alternative is defining your business as an S Corporation (S-Corp). The advantage of an S-Corp is that you pay no income taxes because profits and losses pass through to the shareholders (you). There are specific requirements for defining yourself as an S-Corp for tax purposes, however. I started as the sole member of a limited liability company (LLC) in the State of New York, which allowed me to get a business bank account, and have people write checks to my business instead of me personally. Technically speaking, defining yourself as an LLC allows you to file documents called "articles of organization," which is essentially an operating agreement. If, down the road, other people should become involved in your business, this will be important to have. It gives you the ability to expand eventually, and it also helps you organize your taxes, liability, and compliance.

I'm sure you have additional questions about this, and there are plenty of great sources you can go to for answers. Some popular sites are BizFilings, RocketLawyer, and LegalZoom. No website is a replacement for a real live human looking out for your specific business interests, however. I recommend speaking with a licensed professional if your resources allow it.

Step 2: Make sure you understand your tax and insurance responsibilities

As a business that provides a physically transactional service, you will inevitably expose yourself to a dizzying array of potential liabilities. You need insurance. I recommend that you find a broker you like and stick with him or her. I recommend Professional Liability Coverage, which protects you against financial losses from lawsuits filed against them by their clients.

Good businesses tend to provide insurance for their employees as well, but don't worry about that until after you become better established. If you are covering employees, make sure they fall under the official definition of "employee" as defined by your state. Independent contractors are quite different, and the stakes are high for mistakes here.

Regarding taxes, the state imposes income taxes on corporations, estates, trusts, and individuals. Not every state in the US imposes income taxes on businesses, but most do. Most of us are at the mercy of the Federal Income Tax Code in the running of our businesses, but a good tax accountant can help avoid unnecessary tax pitfalls. Every state and city has its own rules, so do your research. Start with the Website of your local city, town, borough, etc. Then branch out to local, state, and federal government.

Choosing the type of entity to form is dependent upon several factors. These include, but are not limited to, your industry type, number of owners and location. If possible, speaking with a tax specialist for your unique situation can mitigate potential issues down the road if proper planning and initial setup are done correctly.

I don't do any of this. Dan does. In fact, Dan wrote that last sentence above. I have no intention of keeping up with constantly changing rules for compliance and tax calculations, so I have an accountant do my books and taxes. (This is why a business account is essential. You do NOT want this stuff mixed in with personal expenses.) Dan Rackover is my accountant, friend, wartime consigliere – a trusted guardian of my interests. Everybody should have a Dan. We'll get into teams later, but Dan sees things I couldn't possibly understand, and it's an essential expense in my business.

Step 3: Create/Refine your Brand

We have already talked about the brand in a general sense and will talk about it much more as we progress through this book. For now, however, it's essential to realize that branding is marketing. It's a defined entity by which someone wishes to be known--a name, a symbol, a design. In many cases, it is only your name (Ford, Westinghouse, Jordans, Jason Littrell). The critical question to ask is, what does the brand name evoke? What do you think of when you think of Tesla or Michael Kors or Campari? You could probably think of two or three adjectives to describe each brand. Which attributes would you like others to use when describing your brand?

Branding is highly visual, so you might want to design a logo. I recommend Canva or DesignCrowd.com for logo design. It's cheap, and they have many great designs/designers from which to choose. You will be using the same logo for your Website, your Facebook page, Twitter, business cards, etc.

Step 4: Make a Marketing Plan

Trust is everything in marketing.

Before any transaction can occur, trust needs to exist between the customer and the business.

Good marketing builds trust between the suppliers, the company, and the customers. It all starts with a marketing philosophy. Social media democratized marketing, so I'm not suggesting you pay for anything, just have a plan.

Advertising, publicity, and sales technique are what comes to mind when we think about marketing. In truth, marketing and sales are not synonymous. While selling relies on sound marketing, marketing encompasses much more than just selling. Marketing has to do with identifying the right customer segment or the target market, analyzing the needs of your customers, and communicating to them how your product meets their expectations as well as benefits them.

During a startup, most businesses design a marketing strategy to address these issues. It is a long-term strategy intended to keep all elements of the trade in mind. Without marketing, a business is like a road trip in the dark without headlights. Marketing is the beating heart of your business, even before anything turns into sales.

In my case, I depended solely on word of mouth and referrals to support my business and my lifestyle at first. I didn't realize it then, but 60% of my business came from a single client. One year, that client decided to take what I did in-house, and my revenue halved overnight. Hedge your bets, don't put all your eggs in one basket, and always engage a new customer and professional development activities by maintaining a constant presence with new people through marketing and networking and ALWAYS honing your skills. Entrepreneurs read a lot, and I watch a LOT of YouTube videos.

The way you market your service or product depends on how you delight and intrigue your customers, but first, they have to trust you. Trust has become personal in the modern marketing era. It is inseparable from the business. The foundations of the market are dependent on exchanges of trust. People hire people they trust, and people purchase products they can trust. Companies attract their suppliers based on faith. Trust is everything.

It is important to remember the 7-38-55% rule. From two research studies at UCLA, it was understood that feelings and attitudes are communicated 7% by words, 38% by tone of voice, and 55% nonverbally. This means how you articulate your ideas is only 7% of the job. Your voice and tone through which you communicate is 38% of the whole task, and how you present your ideas or manifest them through body language and appearance is 55%. Trust leads to relationships, and the kind of relationships you make will determine your trustworthiness, and thus, your future.

Networking is a fundamental part of doing business. No one makes it in the world alone. You need all the support and backing you can get. Whether you're a chef, bartender, or an event planner, you have to have allies in your field. It works like simple math. The more connections you have, the more comprehensive your reach. The wider your reach, the better your chances of publicity and various opportunities.

The goal is to inform people you know that *this* is your big idea, or *this* is your business.

Tools for Networking

Social media
Google Analytics
Content Marketing
Business Cards

While your market is mainly about the customer, your business is primarily about you. You must build your brand around yourself, infusing it with your individuality while meeting the demands of your customers. You don't want to be just another fish in the sea. Nobody does what you do the way you do it. Nobody.

What sets you apart? How are you different? What makes you distinct?

Before seeking investments in your brand, you have to invest in yourself. Do an honest self-assessment. Know your strengths and weaknesses. Your business exists to solve problems. But you cannot solve every problem, can you? So get specific-- what is your target market, and what their pain points or bottlenecks? What problem needs you to solve it? Do not try to be all things to all people. **The riches are in niches**. It's in your hands to decide which problems you enjoy solving, pick a niche, and market that. If you work on that long enough, you will master that niche. And that's when you later think about expansion. Remember, Google simply started as a search engine.

With my arm in a sling, I had a lot of time to think about what I wanted and how I was going to get it. I didn't know it at the time, but I had taken the first step to be my boss. Owning a business is different than owning a job. It's not easy running a business, but it's yours. Your brand is your professional representation of yourself, rather than a label or a company representing you. When you package your career and your talent to monetize with a businessperson mindset, you create something entirely new. And that's exciting.

Now it's time for me to tell you my story.

Chapter 2

My Story

"The proper work of the mind is the exercise of choice, refusal, yearning, repulsion, preparation, purpose, and assent. What then can pollute and clog the mind's proper functioning? Nothing but its own corrupt decisions."

Epictetus, Discourses, 4.1.6-7

BARTENDER AS A BUSINESS

The bar is about to open. I have missed my bar. Everything is in order. I have set up my vessels so that I can reach for my ingredients in the most efficient order using my most capable hand. I have my measuring tools in place. I'm ready to conceptualize my rounds. I'm pumped.

Customers from all over the world have been waiting for the bar to open, in line for an hour. I have 54 tables and 12 seats at the bar, all of which will be occupied within minutes.

The door host gives me a nod.

The crowds start to come in, first just meandering, then more urgently as the bar fills up. So many faces! I'm smiling. I give the counter a quick wipe as the, just out of an excess of nervous energy. I start talking to bar customers and making drinks for bar customers. I'm listening to that first service ticket. I hear it. Then more and more service tickets come through.

Within minutes, my bar has turned into a MASH unit. I triage the tickets. Will it take 10 seconds or two minutes to make that drink? How many drinks have lime juice? Which ones require the blender? If it's a glass of wine or a beer, it's already gone out. What are the ingredients? What are the measurements of this ingredient? Where is that fucking ingredient? It's a table of eight, and each of those drinks has to come out about the same time, be at the same temperature, they all have to have the correct garnishes and be delivered at the same time.

Tickets are almost to the floor now………..

A round of eight drinks—I stop and conceptualize for 20 seconds—and then take action. Done.

More tickets……..hundreds of tickets………

By this time, hours have gone by. There's no time for a break. Drinks, money and credit cards are everywhere. People are laughing and having a good time. I am in my zone--I could get a million tickets and it wouldn't be a problem.

And then, halfway to sunrise, it's over. Everybody's gone. The front door is closed and locked. I am astonished at what I was able to accomplish during my shift; that feeling never gets old.

I clean my bar and set up my mise for the next shift. Pleased with myself, I stuff my money in my pocket and meet some friends (other bartenders) for a beer and a shot.

My First Job

My first job was a paper route; I was five years old. I know, that's pretty young. Technically, I was helping my Mom with her paper route. And in reality, my whole family delivered papers – Mom, brother, and sister. We would all be out in the garage at 4 a.m. folding papers and then delivering them—every day of the year.

Even though she worked full time, my Mom (being a single mom) was always coming up with schemes to make some extra money. This was just one in a series of her crazy money-making schemes.

At first, I just folded the papers, and then I graduated to folding AND putting rubber bands on. Whenever it rained (not often, this was San Diego), I had to put the papers in plastic bags.

My brother, Johnny, who was five years older, had a bike with a basket on it, so he had his own route. My sister and I helped Mom, who had a car route. Mom would stop the car from time to time, and my sister and I would spread out like cockroaches, delivering as many papers as we could hold while Mom inched the vehicle down the street. It was an old Oldsmobile diesel that my Dad sold to her for cheap. If that obnoxiously-loud diesel engine weren't noisy enough, Mom would also play the car radio real loud. All the neighborhood dogs were barking. I can't believe we weren't arrested.

But we were all together in that garage at 4 a.m. every morning (and I mean 365 mornings a year). Our goal was to get the papers delivered by 5:30 a.m. with no screw-ups because then the phone would ring, and we would have to go back out. Besides, we had to be on the school bus at 6:35 and Mom had to go to work. (God help us if we missed the bus and she had to drive us to school.) It was a tight early-morning schedule and a rather unforgiving introduction to the world of work.

My main memory of this time wasn't the work, but how the papers felt and smelled. I remember my hands and fingers being black at the end of the process. I remember the smell of rubber bands. Something in my exhausted little head was stimulated by the fact that I was executing something….

Even though all child labor law protections were ignored, all I wanted to be was a paperboy. In my mind, if I just had a basket for my bike, I could get my paper route--you know, one of those super big baskets that hold lots of papers. So I would squirrel away my "cut" so I could save for a basket.

Not only did I want my route, but I wanted my own business.

And then one day, the newspaper announced that it was switching to a dispatching system and would no longer have individual carriers, either on bikes or in cars. So we were replaced by a guy with a huge van. It was my first corporate take-over. But something had taken hold inside me.

My first real job was at Boston Market near our house. I wasn't 16 yet, so my Mom had to sign me up for a work permit. I loved having a job, and I remember feeling very proud like I had a role or a purpose. I was so excited to have my ATM card. I remember I put 50 bucks in there. It wasn't much, but it came from a machine. That made it special.

 And I was the only one of my friends that had that.

They wouldn't let me on the cash register at Boston Market, so I just cleaned up after people. The work itself was the worst. But it was mine. One day, I was looking at one of the manager's sheets at what a piece of cornbread costs, and then looking at the menu and seeing what they charged for it. Something clicked. "Oh, okay. They're not doing this for fun." So that was an exciting thing to take away from that.

I got my driver's license on my 16th birthday—a pivotal step towards independence. I started planning how to get through high school in three years. It was a stable and nourishing upbringing, but still, I wanted to get the fuck out. I just didn't like the idea of having to do what other people told me to do. I had no interest in learning about weird and esoteric mathematic applications. So I did what I had to do--I took courses at a community college even though I hated it. I didn't get the grades (I sucked at school), but I got the credits, so I was able to get myself graduated from the job pipeline.

During that time, I was a pretty serious drummer. I was practicing the drums 6-8 hours a day, sometimes in a hot, dark, stinky garage. The lady across the street would yell at me, or bring her radio out to the front yard and turn it up real loud, just to piss me off – as if I would notice. I liked drumming a lot, I didn't realize it until much later, but while I was in love with music, I wasn't in love with being broke all the time. I studied music in college (for about five minutes), but it slowly and painfully dawned on me that music was going to be a struggle for the rest of my life, no matter how good I was. That didn't appeal.

Becoming a Bartender

I had a series of silly little jobs until I finally got a job that pointed me in the right direction. I got a job as a busboy at a restaurant called Hooley's, near Mom's house in East County, San Diego. I worked for a batshit crazy manager, an Irishman named Tommy Dowd, who was my first real mentor and still is to this day. Tommy would fly off the handle, alternating between very angry and very loving. I learned a lot from him, and I still seek his counsel.

Hooley's was a great job except for one big problem. I wanted to be a bartender, and I was willing to do whatever I had to do to earn that. I told everybody. I started out washing dishes, and then I bussed tables, and eventually, I became a server.

Around my 21st birthday, I went to the owner and told him that I wanted to be a bartender. My understanding was that they only wanted women behind the bar, and it was a very stable job, so there was not a lot of churn with the bartenders. So I quit. I told him I would have been the best bartender he ever had. And who knows, if I got that job, I might still be there. So, thank you, Craig.

The next week, I got a bartender job at Shooter's Cocktails down the street, which was a defining time in my career. That place was a fucking dump. What a rough and tumble place. Drug deals in the parking lot happened regularly. Rumor has it—and I'm pretty sure this was true—that I replaced the day bartender who had gotten stabbed by one of the customers. My foot was in the door. I worked from 10 to 6 Monday through Friday. I was always on time. It was the day shift, so how much trouble could I possibly get into? Trailer parks surrounded Shooters, so people who lived in the trailer parks would come in. They would put all their available cash on the bar, and just keep drinking until all the liquid was gone. It was all regulars, and none of them had money. This bar was a time machine. Time was suspended.

This one guy, Mule, would come in, and he would drink $2 Budweisers. He would always drink 10 of them on that $20 bill that he put down in front of me. Never said a word, ever. (Joe, the owner of the place, said, "He drinks Bud." That's how I knew.) He never looked at me. He didn't even leave his barstool to pee. He would regularly eliminate in his barstool. Guess who had to clean that up every day. He would come in smelling like piss, and he would leave smelling like piss. And he did the same thing precisely every day. He came in every day for about two months, and I don't know what happened to him after that. Without a word, this shellshocked vet taught me about humility.

Rock and Roll

One day, I got a call to be a drummer in LA. I wasn't going anywhere at Shooter's, and I could stay with my brother in his rent-controlled apartment in LA, so I jumped at the chance. Somehow, I got a job with a radio station—KBIG 104/KOST103 --and also worked for Red Bull, driving that stupid little car around. And I was playing music. I was gigging around LA at the time, making some in-roads, some connections, playing with some bands fairly regularly, living hand to mouth the whole time, living to play with bands.

Around this time, my friend Marc from high school (a budding young pop star), called and he said, "I'm going on tour! Be my tour manager! (Actually, it was "Can you come down and be our merch guy?") So I quit all of my jobs and started driving a Suburban across the country. This car, a subsequent Winnebago, hotel rooms, couches, and floors, became my home for two and a half years.

Marc's band was on the Warped Tour, and they thought that that was a path to success and riches. For a while, it could have been. After the Warped Tour, they would play gigs at small rock clubs around the country in front of anywhere from 5 to a thousand teenagers. I remember packing everything up, driving to San Diego, picking up the van, and then leaving the next morning to drive from San Diego to Buffalo, NY. I ended up getting promoted to Tour Manager after the last one moved on. I was 23. It was an adventure. I didn't have much responsibility, and I saw new towns and cities every day. All I had to do was drive when it was my turn and sell shirts for the band, pack up and haul gear, and occasionally contact the next venue to advance our arrival.

Considering the twelve thousand miles we were driving a month, there were, of course, some problems. I remember waiting a week for a new transmission in New London, Connecticut. It was like a carny, and it was terrific--until the band's funding ran out.

Next thing I knew, I was back living at home with Mom.

New York

The good news was, I was still working with Marc, and we were again playing some shows like our band Bedford Grove in San Diego when some connections with New York came about. So we headed to New York to record an album, and to see what might happen.

We were supposed to be in New York for three months. I had $175 in the bank, and an old high school friend of mine was walking dogs here, and she said she would help me get a job. So literally the first full day I was here, I was making $10/hour walking dogs around Washington Square Park. At that time, I was living on a couch on Grove Street in the West Village with a dear and unbelievably generous friend, Jen.

The plan was this; Marc was in charge of writing the music, and I would work walking dogs every day. At night, we recorded. It was a different world then, and we were focused on perfect; when done, would have been just fine. We lived a pretty meager existence. Marc's friend Cameron from the old neighborhood would come over a lot and cook incredible meals because he was in culinary school here (he ended up being a baker at Per Se, and now owns a taco shop in Los Angeles). Marc never had any intention of staying in New York. And the time eventually came when it was time for him to move on. I had fallen in love with New York.

By this time, I had made good friends in New York. And, from a future-facing perspective, I didn't have much to go back to in San Diego. Honestly, I'm pretty sure at the time, the reason I didn't go back to San Diego was that I couldn't afford it. I had no money. I had nothing except my drums. I had the clothes on my back and a bag full of stuff, and that was it. But I never even thought of going home. I don't remember ever thinking, "Can you go back to San Diego? This is kicking my ass; I've got to go back." New York just lives and breathes energy. It's everywhere. People in San Diego work to live. People here live to work. I always felt that I would be able to find a delicate balance here where I could have a nice hustle and generate opportunities for myself in music. But I could also have a smaller footprint where I could be agile enough to take chances as they came.

At this point, all I could hope for was to hang in there and know that something would break open eventually. It wasn't even a question. I have never heard a story where somebody said, "I came to New York to play music, and everything worked out great, and now I'm rich and famous." I never expected for a second that it would be easy. And I never really cared about being rich or famous. And I knew that it was not a natural lifestyle choice (college *might* have been more comfortable in retrospect), and you just kind of have to roll with it. Eventually, you find your place.

The end of my music career involved living in a dumpy Yonkers apartment, paying rent, then getting locked out of my apartment because the mortgage wasn't being satisfied. I was no longer a drummer. I don't remember where I slept that night.

Coming Up

My first bartender job in New York was at Cafetasia on East 6th and University by NYU. I got that job because I manufactured a resume that had New York experience on it. I was the first bar manager there. I made $50/week.

I was a great bartender, but a terrible mixologist. But I learned, and I got better. This bar was in the heart of NYU, so everybody just drank beer anyway. But I would put together these little drink menus that were not that good, and they tasted terrible because nobody had shown me how to make drinks and I didn't know anything.

That was enough experience to get me into a very famous live music venue in Times Square. This is where I learned to be fast behind the bar. There were no barbacks on that job, so you had to do everything. And to work the good shifts, you had to work the shitty shifts, and that's how it balanced out. So you would have to work lunch during the day, which was extremely slow, and you prepped all the garnish for the night shift. That's when I started making $600-$700/night. For the first time, I was beginning to put money in my pocket and get comfortable. And then I got fired.

I got fired because I violated some policy that I wasn't aware of about exchanging tips. In casino parlance, I was coloring up. My drawer was perfectly fine. Depending on the show, we would have 2-10 bartenders behind the bar. Each of us had our register. And so I would ring $6,000 - $7,000 on my register every night, and we would need to get change from the managers so that we would have singles in our drawers. We weren't supposed to do that ourselves. But I remember one night thinking, "I can't sell anything because I don't have any change to give these people." So I exchanged the tips out of my drawer to have singles so I could keep ringing.

At this large, high-volume venue, you didn't even count your tips, which was shady as shit. There were cameras everywhere, including on each drawer. We always checked out in triplicate. On this particular night, my bank was counted, my money was good, and that was checked out with paperwork, and then it was checked out again with the controller the next day when they accounted for the day's sales. Weeks later, the boss came up to me and said, "We saw that you were cheating."

They told me my register was $1,000 short. They said, sign this piece of paper saying you stole $1,000 from us, and we won't call the cops on you. And I said, "That's crazy, look at the camera. Yes, I did. I was forced to do this. I took $20 out, and I put $20. The drawer was never short."

My drawer was spot on that night, and I have never cheated an employer. I knew that I didn't steal anything. But they insisted, saying we have you on camera, we saw you take $1,000. And I said that's crazy. Look at the camera again. I never stole anything. They said we have a policy where you can't have shifts. And I said, I never heard about this policy. I never signed anything to that effect. And they said, well we do. Then they said, "We saw you stealing tips out of the tip jar. Sign this paper, and we won't call the cops." I was shitting my pants.

I ended up signing this piece of paper because I was too scared not to, and that's probably the thing I regret the most – in my entire career in hospitality. I should have stood my ground and said, "Fuck you, prove it." But if I had gotten arrested, I would have had to go to jail that night. I had no money because I had just signed a lease for my first apartment.

I signed and walked away. They were threatening my freedom, and that's the thing I value the most. It was not a proud moment. I just feel like that document is going to show up one day, and I'm going to say, "Why did I sign that......?" It bothers me greatly that this document exists somewhere even though they are no longer in business.

That was the end of that chapter.

I got a job at a place called Dip, a fondue bar, a very redeeming experience. The folks there actually gave a shit about me, and for a change, I was working for people who were genuinely interested in whether I lived or died. In my interview, I told them why I got fired, and they said, "That's awful, you got the job." Because they knew I was honest.

I don't feel bad about lying on my first resume to get my job because I knew I could prove myself as being worth the risk. But that should have been the last dishonest thing I ever did. The only other false thing I've ever done behind a bar was sign that fucking paper.

At Dip, I worked with a guy named Bobby, and he got me a job at this place called The Randolph. It was the best job in the world.

NOLITA

The Randolph had gone through a few iterations over the years. When I started working there, it was dark and gritty. But there was a time in downtown New York when people were really into underground, grungy scenes. Soon to be famous, DJs used to come in there and spin because it seemed like there were no rules. The doors would open at 9 or 10, and I would roll in there, start making drinks at 11, work until 6 a.m., and leave with $1,000. The drinks were simple, and people drank recklessly. Thursday through Saturday I worked the only open three days of the week, I would destroy myself—working my ass off and drinking a lot. The other four days a week, I would read the paper, live a quiet life, have hobbies, read books. I was making $3,000 a week.

The Randolph was below a hotel. We were loud. Whenever somebody complained at the hotel above the Randolph, they would be forced to comp the room. This got old, very fast.

My bosses Hari and Dave were running the show then, and they were both brilliant numbers guys. Their projections indicated it would be more profitable for them to open up the bar for longer hours during the day, seven days a week, and taking the risk of joining the burgeoning cocktail revolution happening in New York around 2007.

Who better to usher this in than the immutable godfather of the US Cocktail revival, Mr. Sasha Petraske?

The Randolph became a cocktail bar. Because we were open late, it also became known as a bartender's bar. I actively cultivated this by serving a ton of beer. We were capable of serving a staggering array of classics, but bartenders came to tell war stories and have a lowkey shot and a beer. The last thing you want after making fancy cocktails for 12 hours is a fancy cocktail. You just want a shot and a beer. We happily obliged.

I drank a lot at that time. When I wasn't drinking, I was studying. I started studying drinks because I was afraid I wouldn't know what people would ask for that night. I still have my box full of flashcards...a record of other people's menus, ingredients, variations, classics, and a continued string of my laughable creations.

Word got out that I knew my drinks, so bartenders would come in to try to stump me. They did. They would run me through my paces and see if I knew anything. I didn't. They would say, "What did Sasha teach you? I was just completely fascinated with this new world of drinks and the world of cocktails. People came to realize that I gave a shit. I think that's why they enjoyed busting my chops so hard because they kept on asking for the more obscure drinks.

The Randolph was the industry darling for a year, which is a long time. I was a terrible bar manager, but I think the bar did OK.   The price of our drinks was unheard of for that bar, in that neighborhood at that time, especially for a place that wasn't precisely polished, but in reality, the drinks were free. People paid to stay.

After two great years, I had reached the peak of my contribution. I was the one who was supposed to be innovating, but I was never actually wildly creative with cocktails. I was working at three different places very briefly—Randolph, Cain (a Chelsea nightclub), and I had started training at Death & Co.

Death and Co

Dave Kaplan, the owner of Death & Co was a regular at the Randolph. At one point, every bartender had gone to the Randolph several times. I found out that one of the bartenders at Death & Co, Alex Day, was going to be leaving. Unbeknownst to me, I was being scouted and vetted to replace him. At this point, music was a distant memory, and I had chosen my path. For the first time, I was looking at tending bar as a community and a career.

Death & Co was like joining the Yankees. The money from the nightclub was great and allowed me to train several nights a week at Death & Co. Just training with Alex Day, Brian Miller, Jessica Gonzalez, Joaquin Simo, Jillian Vose, and Thomas Waugh was one of the highest honors of my career. I trained whenever they would allow me to because I knew I had a long way to go to qualify for a shift and meet the minimum requirements to work at this legendary bar.

My training period at Death & Co was around six weeks. It was the most I had learned in the shortest period of my life. My education was far more comprehensive than just building drinks. It was a philosophy, and a mission.

Alex Day is the most technical bartender I had ever seen — more cocktail and design engineer, than bartender -- but still wildly approachable and positive. Alex and Dave built a specimen of operational efficiency in the scaled expansion of Death & Co across several markets.

Jason Littrell

Brian Miller was the fun uncle who's understated depth of knowledge of cocktail theory was sometimes masked by eye makeup, a sarong, and a signature Keith Richards vibe.

Thomas Waugh was my boss for the longest time during my tenure, and his limitless creativity in cocktail concepts constantly challenged the prevailing "Mr. Potatohead" methodology of simply exchanging one ingredient for another and calling it a new thing.

Jessica Gonzalez was another invaluable teacher whos rigid and exacting standards exemplified the detail and precision I would later use to run my business.

Joaquin Simo, was a deep thinker. While our shifts together were not numerous, they were impactful. I remember the questions and thoughts he offered during cocktail R&D sessions, and there was another dimension of theoretical intensity I had not considered. I was working with crayons and coloring books, he was working with string theory.

While I have this opportunity, I think it's important to mention the incredible work of the barbacks and kitchen teams at Death & Co. They kept the engine running, while the bartenders and servers drove the car.

BARTENDER AS A BUSINESS

The best example is Dave Powell. At that time, he was a barback, but Dave was always a star. He and I always had this connection. Dave anticipated. We flowed. It's no mystery how he leveraged these skills to run bars and eventually be a brand leader on the national stage.

A fun story that I never get to live down is how I 'trained' Jillian Vose when she first started at the bar. I was arrogant, condescending, and thought I knew everything. I was wrong. Jillian became my boss a few weeks later.

This education was immersive and diverse. Sometimes I would show up unexpectedly, and I would just go in to train. Whenever they needed a barback, and I would go to work, years after my last shift, I would still pick up a barback, door, or sometimes even a bar shift (not that that's a menu you can just walk in and execute). They were extremely loyal to me, and I continue to be extremely loyal to them.

I finally got my first shifts -- Sundays and Tuesdays. Sundays were like Gladiator School. Sundays at that time were easily the hardest shift because you work the first two hours by yourself. I would get there at 4 p.m., set up the bar by 6. The bar would open at 6, and the next bartender wouldn't get there until 8. And you would work through the entire shift until closing.

Jason Littrell

4-6 was set-up. It was establishing your mise—
cutting garnishes, making sure all of your tools are
clean everywhere, making sure that all of your
syrups were prepped and prepared, your infusions
were done, etc. The opening bartenders did all
that. Busy is relative at a place that is seating only.
"Busy" is a matter of the rate that people drink, not
the number of people who show up. By law and by
concept, there were only so many people who can
fit in there. There's no standing room or transient
people. At the time, there was a doorman, so you
can't just walk in and seat yourself. A door person
greeted guests and would typically ask, "how many
in your party? We should have a seat in about 20
minutes. What's your phone number? We'll give
you a call when this is ready." So in case
something happens, a machine breaks down, a
bartender hurts themself, or we're limited to one
bartender, they will limit how many people can
come in. And they will pace out the door for you,
which is what a good door person does there. The
door host is keenly aware of when the check is
being dropped on the table, and they'll call the
person and say, "your table is going to be ready in
ten minutes."

At six o'clock, there was a line on the sidewalk.
There are 54 seats total, and 12 of those are at the
actual bar. So that would mean that every seat
would fill up at 6 o'clock, and you would get 54
drink orders. And you had to put those in order

and triage. Up first were things that you could get out fast. The server could take one order, then bring it back and then take another order. So the time that it took to make another order, that was the time you had to execute your round. Otherwise, you would get backed up.

It wasn't uncommon to work 10 hours without going to the bathroom or eating anything. It doesn't matter. You don't think about it. You're in combat mode. You're just ready to go.

There are two stations at Death & Co--point and service. Service is the 44 seats out there. And the point only serves the 12 seats, ...which is plenty with 60 something drinks on the menu. And if you're behind on service, they'll pick up a few tickets and help you bang some out. But I like to go to service just because it's much more comfortable, much more efficient not to have to talk to people or touch money. I didn't mind talking to people. I loved it. But if I were going to talk to people, I would rather only deal with those 12 seats rather than do service tickets. What you do is you do three or four tables in rapid succession. You stack orders. If there is a table of two and a table of six people, you will try to find out the common ingredients of the two tables. Say there are seven drinks total. You would find out what the common ingredients were and only pick up that one bottle once. And then you would lay out seven vessels to make drinks in.

Jason Littrell

You're constantly thinking about efficiency. How
can I save a step here? And it gets to the point
where you end up visualizing your round that
comes into your head. Say you have a daiquiri, a
margarita, a Manhattan and an old-fashioned. The
daiquiri and the margarita both have lime juice and
they're both shaken too. So you put lime juice, and
any other citrus that you need, shake with both
hands......You can shake one drink and stir two
drinks at one time, you can stir four drinks at a
time, you can shake two drinks at a time, there are
a lot of little efficiencies. But keep in mind that all
these drinks have to finish at exactly the same
time. And if they are served on the ice, they have
to arrive at the table without being too diluted.
And everything was tasted twice.

We would have three to four menus a year – so
you have to learn 30-40 new drinks on a 50-60
drink menu, but you also had to learn where
everything was, the exact measurements of the
cocktails down to the half-teaspoon or drop, and
you had to learn what the pacing of these cocktails
was. If the air conditioner broke down, your ice
would be wet, which meant that – and that
happened regularly in the old days – people would
perceive the drink as being warmer. So you had to
do things like pull out the glass last while it was still
frozen just before the drink was finished. There
are a million different variables.

BARTENDER AS A BUSINESS

At Death & Co is where I first learned about dealing with drops, teaspoons, half teaspoons, rinses, and the obsessive process of consistently defending the mantle of a world class cocktail bar to an international audience. It was here that I learned the power of process and intensity.

I worked at Death & Co a little over two years. The money was not phenomenal there, but it was extremely consistent. The perception on the way you tip on a remarkable dish is not the same way you tip on a phenomenal drink. People still perceive that $1 a drink is reasonable, and that's regularly what we got. But our capacity to make drinks was about 300 drinks a night. That's a good living wage in New York. Just like anything else, the drinks were phenomenal, sometimes we got incredible tips, sometimes we got shit tips. We got paid, some days were great, some days were not-so-great. But you take home money every night and you don't have to think about it the minute you leave the door. You made your drinks, you got your cash, and you walked away.

Even in the most phenomenal bar in the world, I was still just a shift worker--and always would be. It was just a job, but it gave rise to a career. A career built on the skills I learned behind bars.

Independent Consulting

I started at Death & Co in 2008. In 2010, I started (and concurrently operated) my company, Critical Mass Events, LLC. Eventually, I was getting work putting events together. I was about 30 at the time, and I had been doing this for a while, long enough to understand the mortality of bartenders and the physical demands of it.

Critical Mass lost money in the first year, broke even in the second year, and was my full-time job the third year. It was like a plant I watered and it grew. Was it easy? No, Was it interesting and fun? Yep. And I learned resilience and problem solving that I would never have learned. By its fourth year, it grossed a half a million dollars in sales. Do I get to keep all that? No, but it's still a decent living, and 100% on my own terms.

It was hard to manage my brand, run my business, to put in work overdrunk on coffee without any guarantee if it will pay off. It was scary, but it was MINE. With at-will employment, you may not have a job tomorrow anyway. There is no more risk in filing an LLC than there is in working a shift or hourly job. You're ALREADY an entrepreneur, and with your business, you've decided to set your foot into the field of your niche that you can own.

Chapter 3

Discovering Your Brand

The rest of this book is about you.

The purpose of this chapter will motivate
you to believe in your skills, your
experience, your people skills--in all aspects
of yourself--and will help you monetize the
whole package and turn you into a brand.

Not sure what the difference between a
brand and a business is? We'll start by
discussing value proposition and how top
individuals and businesses showcase theirs.
We will also look at the distinctions and
interconnectedness between businesses
and brands. In looking at some of the most

successful personal brands out there and soaking in what can be learned from their journeys and profiles, you will be well-positioned to start building a brand and a business for you.

What Lights Your Fire?

You're not a shrimping boat captain, ping pong champion and a philanthropist. Neither are you a painter, sculptor, humanist, scientist, architect, philosopher and an engineer like Leonardo da Vinci. You may not design the next Taj Mahal or launch a successful plan for the conquest of Mars. You don't need to be these people. You already possess a set of skills that determine your value as a unique individual. You don't need to compare yourself against the most accomplished people who have EVER lived.

When is the last time you attended an awards banquet for hospitality workers? Has your employer given you a huge annual bonus for exemplary performance on the line this year? I didn't think so. You don't enjoy the recognition or prestige that high-end professions take for granted.

But that doesn't mean you're not a genius. Albert Einstein said, "Everybody is a genius.

But if you judge a fish by its ability to climb a tree, it will live its whole life believing that it is stupid." If you love what you do, you should follow it with as much passion as one would follow, for instance, painting, singing, architecture or physics.

There's nothing wrong with achievement. But, personally, I think it is over-valued in our society; being a person of integrity and doing what you love is where it's at for me. How many people compromise what they love to become an engineer or a doctor? You didn't do that--and I'm going to make you glad you didn't. Your happiness and personal autonomy is much more important.

Since your adolescence at least, you have noticed something unique about you as compared to other people. That thing that makes you different from other people is the very thing we are focused on here. It is the kernel of who you are, and you are going to be happy only if you do what it tells you to do. Now.

On the other hand, if you think you don't have any talent, you need to look closer. Come up with something unique, even if it is a small thing. Do it now. You may be someone who is great at scrutinizing the marketing and business tactics by reading advertising and marketing, or you may be great at being talkative and can go around compiling different ideas about fashion trends. Begin by identifying these traits and recognizing how they make you different. You can capitalize on these skills to establish a brand of your own. <u>This belief becomes an attitude that becomes your brand, which leads to your success</u>. As Margaret Atwood wrote, "You may not be able to alter reality, but you can alter your attitude towards it, and this, paradoxically, alters reality. Try it and see."

You can monetize your skills anytime you like. It's like having a credit card in your pocket except you won't get a bill. People before you have done it. They continue to do it today. The idea is to take a chance and find a way. Keep trying. There are countless innovators and entrepreneurs who never dreamed they would become as big as they have become. With all humility, I was one of those. Nobody will know your value unless you do. So know your value.

After you figure out what you're good at, then figure out what you're not good at. Then study your market. What does it need? What are its pain points? There is always a new, creative spin to a niche within a field that nobody has thought of. There is a way to appeal to the customer no one has ever tried. A strategy, a technique, a lock nobody has the key to. It is as inevitable as your uniqueness, difficult to find but certainly there. What rock has not yet been turned over?

How to Identify your Value Proposition

- Identify what you are good at.
- Identify what else needs to be done.

- Study the market to determine what it needs.

- Put together a plan to meet the needs of the market.

Do you see it? Congratulations, you have just unlocked your value proposition, your business, and your brand.

For more on Value Proposition, head to learn.jlittrell.com and sign up for a free course.

The Difference between Brand and Business

Your brand and your business are separate but intertwined. While your business is the agent of your product, your brand is your image, voice, and your style. The two can, however, overlap. There could be a brand that is also a company. (Think Pepsi.)

Pay more attention to your personal brand because it transcends your business brand – at least in the beginning. What does this mean? For a long time it was difficult for me to say the words "Personal Brand" out loud. If you want to get in business for yourself, you become the brand. So get over it.

Your business is the entity that receives money, pays taxes, and can be sold. But you are the brand. You are not going to get into tax trouble as a brand, but your business might. Your brand is how you represent yourself; YOU are going to appear on a morning show, not your business. Branding yourself means becoming the face of your services and product. It's important to understand how these two things are different, and what their relationship is to one another.

Brand on Fire

Let us look at some famous chefs and bartenders who have established themselves as personal brands: Emeril Lagasse, Guy Fieri, and Charles Joly.

Emeril Lagasse

Emeril Lagasse is known as the favorite son of Food Television Network, whose show 'Essence of Emeril' premiered in 1995. Known by millions only by his first name, Emeril's contributions to professional cooking--especially the "masculinization" of cooking--are legion. Emeril had the nascent Food TV Network's top-rated show when it debuted and, the very next year, *Time Magazine* named Essence of Emeril one of the best television shows of 1996. This was unheard of for a show from an obscure niche cable network. Bam!

When you are that good, business comes looking for you. Emeril's raging popularity earned him the second show called Emeril Live in 1997. This time he wasn't just cooking; he had a band, a studio audience and celebrity guests. The award-winning Emeril Live became one of the most popular programs ever on FoodTV.

Emeril is an icon today, at one point receiving 775,000 requests for seats in the 2000-seat capacity audience for his live shows. Marquee Brands spent $215 million to acquire him, and eventually, Martha Stewart from Sequential Brands acquired him from Marquee Brands. Emeril's visit to a Detroit restaurant was second only to Bill Clinton's visit in crowd size.

With more than 15 cookbooks and 76,000 entries on Google, products bearing his name in grocery stores across the world, Emeril has become a major brand. Some of his catchphrases, such as "kick it up another notch," "pork fat rules," and the widespread "BAM!" are spoken on a regular basis by Americans.

Guy Fieri

Guy Fieri is the host of the single most popular show on the Food Network, *Diners, Drive-Ins, and Dives*. The 'Chef-dude' has hosted game shows, received Emmy awards, and attracts more male audience than any other prime-time show. With his signature spikey bleached-blond hair and sunglasses resting on the back of his neck, Guy is cool enough to make you want to sit down with him about anything. He laughs,

he talks, he is loud. His cooking is loud too –
in contrast with the calm and profession
style of Emeril - with his restaurants
offering mouth-watering menu items such
as 'Artichoke Hearts' and 'Jackass Roll.'

Fieri's brand is not just an outgoing
personality (although he has one). He
comes across as authentic, original, lovable,
confident, and audacious. He wasn't
created from focus group data or
continuous censoring. He is
unapologetically himself. Blaine Parker aptly
describes him as *"a tattooed nutcase with a
kitchen ladle,"* That's Guy Fieri, the iconic
brand.

Fieri is a popular punching bag and butt of
jokes, but as a business, I have a lot of
respect for him. He also appears to have
extremely wholesome progressive values,
which I also appreciate. Git that a google
search.

Charles Joly

"My personal brand built very organically over
more than a decade in cocktail specific
environments. When we were doing competitions
in the 2000s, it was just to meet other like-minded
individuals and get out of our comfort zones, while

maybe winning the chance to travel. Right place, right time, right work ethic. The side effect was definitely making a lot of connections and getting my name out there.

Being a good media partner helped a lot as well- they come back to you when you make it easy for them.   World Class was certainly a game-changer, it pivoted everything. Completely unplanned, we launched Crafthouse Cocktails right around the same time.

My time at the Aviary helped both myself and that venue in different ways. When we won the James Beard Award for Outstanding Beverage Program, it was only the second year that the category even existed. It marked a change in the way the culinary community looked at the bar portion of the business. To be seen by the most elite restaurateurs as a category to be recognized, where wine has always been king was very cool."

Charles Joly was the first American to win the World Class Bartender of the Year award in 2014. Beating out 11,000 participants from 50 countries – inarguably one of the highest achievements attainable as a bartender.

You would think that Charley Joly was simply a remarkable bartender who was lightning-quick and mixed drinks to flavor perfection. But this was not all of it. His obvious aptitude, his charm, his creativity and hospitable emotional intelligence were what did it. He won on brand. His brand never forgot his humble beginnings in an array of clubs, high volume concepts and party bars that lead to cocktail bars, all the while making meaningful connections with his guests.

Charles has been working in the industry since 2001, climbing up the ladder from part-time to full-time, as many of us do. He eventually became the co-founder of a ready to drink cocktail brand Crafthouse, which flirted with the multi-billion dollar conglomerate Constellation Brands' incubator. Additionally, his brand Crafthouse by Fortessa offers high end barware and glassware. This is hustle.

What do Legasse, Fieri, and Joly have in common?

It is clear to us that style and image in line with the personal brand directs the individual's success. Companies are attracted to the brand because of these qualities. It could make them want to rent your brand or co-opt your style in their image. This is why it's important to develop your personal brand, and style, because this may be the precise element your potential client is missing and wants.

The personal brand begins with the brand owner. Are you the next Emeril?

What do these three individuals have in common?

- Passion for excellence
- Authenticity and honesty
- Great style and image
- Tremendous people skills
- Willingness to be mentored
- High tolerance for hard work
- Openness to recognize opportunities when they come along

Personal Brand and Value Proposition

It is these elements, or **value propositions,** that HAVE to be identified before any truly effective advertising campaign can be developed.

Say you have identified your skills and passion and know what you want to do with your life. That is good news, and congratulations are in order! But you need more. You may have a command over bartending or cooking, but what is unique about you on a molecular level? Why are you, irreplaceable? How do your skills manifest in a manner that nobody else's does? Yes, you may be someone who can juggle multiple bottles of drinks while serving, or ambidextrously cook, bake, blend, and compose food poetry. But this is not what will ultimately set you apart. What sets you apart is your style; how you make your skill come to life.

Let's say, for example, that I can stir four drinks at the same time. While this gives me bragging rights in a job interview, it is not the thing that sets the *quality* of my drinks apart. My Manhattan has to taste really good too. If I can stir drinks better than others AND have it taste better than the standard, that would be unique.

But that's still not enough.

Let's say your personal hot shit technique stands apart from others because you added a special bitters blend that lends a mysteriously good (and BETTER) flavor. As a result of this unconventional style/technique, the customers come to love your Manhattan so much that it becomes your signature dish. You could similarly have an array of cocktails, through uncanny experimentations, result in establishing your unique style and name. This is not limited to drinks. This is how I run my business.

Your **value proposition** is your set of unique strengths, your strategy for pulling the customers towards you, again and again, and again. This makes you special. This way, <u>you can use your personal brand to set a value proposition to sell your services more efficiently than those who do not brand themselves</u>.

If you excel while working at a restaurant or bar, the credit goes to the bar. But with personal branding and your (side) hustle, the credit goes to you.

How I Found my Value Proposition

In the beginning, the value of my brand was tied to the brand of the bar I worked at. The credit that was my due would get projected to the bar, and rightfully so for training me. People assumed I was good at what I did because I worked at a reputable bar – admittedly, that wasn't necessarily true. If you had seen other bartenders at the bar and compared them with me, you'd see the real picture. My talents were different from the bartenders who worked there. I was more creative in other areas. You would have found me a warm, hospitable, personable, and humble (ha!)

bartender. This value was transferred intrinsically to my employers.

Business Brand and Value Proposition

Once you become a business, you will continuously be focused on value proposition. Value proposition does for the customers what candy does for kids, attracts them like a magnet. Your business' value proposition is the most important element of the overall messaging your business should broadcast. Value proposition not only sets the business apart from other businesses providing the same service, but it also lures customers psychologically. These are some of the famous examples of how they do it.

The Uber Shade: Uber has been criticized by its driver employees and customers for depriving them of their rights and protection and has been under the government's radar for its unethical tax-avoiding policies. Yet, you cannot deny it, it is the largest multinational transportation network company. Uber's name has become a part of people's everyday lingo. We don't talk about taking the taxi anymore. We talk about taking an Uber.

And this game-changing convenience makes Uber special and becomes its value proposition.

Uber has changed the way public transportation works. The homepage of its website talks about the Uber convenience in the simple three lines:

One tap and a car comes directly to you

Your driver knows exactly where to go

Payment is completely cashless

If you look at these three lines closely, you realize that they are not only about the superior Uber services, but also about eliminating the things that are bad about the traditional taxi. By not saying it, the company says that in a taxi, you have to approach the car, help the driver navigate and pay out of hand. All these things are micro-stresses. The slogan highlights Uber's efficiency, which is backed by the wonders of technology. So when this company writes, "Your day belongs to you," at the top of their webpage, they're sort of right.

The Apple Appeal: Unsurprisingly, Apple not only has a number of value propositions, but also a dramatic way of marketing them. Most companies couldn't pull off using words such as "magical" to describe their products, but Apple can. And then they get us to do it for them.

Some value propositions of Apple are its range of products, the design, the fluid touch and inventiveness of features like fingerprint scanner and face unlock. Apple's value proposition is the *Apple Experience*.

Apple believes a phone "should be more than a collection of features" – but a smartphone is nothing more than that. Focusing on their features in a romantically in a brutally competitive market works for Apple. You are at the end left with an *"I've got to get myself the new iPhone,"* feeling; it doesn't matter if you've just bought one.

Apple makes it so that it is not really the device you need, because that you can get from another company cheaper. The device represents something else. And that is what you want, enhanced *Apple experience.* Apple's value proposition.

We have seen individual and collective approaches to value proposition in branding and business. I hope these ideas inspire you to think about your or your business' value proposition.

We have also seen that you already have the necessary skills to start your own brand. We have also understood the importance of this startup and seen examples of how other entrepreneurs have applied their value propositions to their respective brands and companies. We have briefly discussed the distinction between brand and business too - though you are inseparable, you complement each other.

In your personal brand, the value proposition is what you are bringing to the brand. It is your uniqueness

Now that you understand your brand and your company, let's dive right into to planning. What's next?

Chapter 4

Understanding Your Business

After clearing up the distinctions between your business and your personal brand, we will now focus on your business in this chapter, particularly on the importance of understanding your business before you even start it. We will talk about how and why knowledge and understanding is critical. We will explore ideas--where do they come from? I will share with you some general ideas to leverage your existing skills into added value in the world of hospitality, event management, PR, distribution, or WHATEVER and help you understand the importance of creating a niche out of one or more of them.

Doing Your Research

Being in business is not merely hard work. Hard work is, in fact, backed up by smart work. What we are about to explore will require you to become a student again and think in terms of **research**.

You don't dive head-first straight into a business; that approach (or rather lack of approach) is for the irrational and the impatient among us. That's what I did, and I paid the price later. The first step toward building a business is understanding what your business is all about and what it does.

This goes without saying (almost): *Before thinking about starting a business, you must excel at your job*. Invest in your education, and experience. If your research about your business doesn't lead to something interesting, the services and products you offer in your business won't be either. Excel at your job, then do the research. Or do both at the same time.

Many up-and-comers skip these steps and they get frustrated later. They thought they had everything sorted out. They had a passion for it, they had the right skills, and they may have even had the network. But all of these are empty without the foundations of knowledge: commitment to excellence and continuing skills development.

The Knowledge is Already There

By research, I don't mean the kind that keeps you Googling until your eyes bleed. You don't have to attend expensive hospitality services workshops either. If you are rabidly intense at what you do, and are starving for more information, you can't make a mistake. Make a mentor out of everyone.

Things to Ask a Mentor

- What is your experience and how did you get to where you are?
- How does your business operate, and how did you grow?
- What are the SYSTEMS and habits that lead to your success?
- What are your aspirations for the future?

Interview everybody, you know. And don't limit yourself to your own employer or friends; help from similar businesses or businesses in entirely different fields is also a good idea. Who knows what may pop out to you, your "aha" moment is out there somewhere.

Learning on the Job

One thing is clear. No matter what your role or your industry is, understanding the business environment you are seeking to join is crucial. Here are several key tips for maximizing your learning while you are still at your current job:

Tip #1: Interview everybody: We have seen that the first step in thriving as a business is thriving at your job; not surprisingly, you tend to thrive at your job by learning about your business. Resolve to learn as much about your current business as you can. And do it now--a new start, a new opportunity you are giving yourself will hopefully **create energy** and excitement. Talk to whomever you can pin down about all aspects of their path and business.

You already are an insider; you work there. You already have access to the information about your business. What a perfect place to start! Become an expert about this one particular place of employment.

The next step is deciding whom to interview. By "interview," I don't mean an up-close and personal interview with microphones and cameras. I'm talking about a casual but substantive conversation with anybody who will talk to you.

Tip #2: Find a Mentor: You may be brilliant at the work you do, but you are not brilliant at all aspects of the business. Say you don't know much about marketing, event or brand management. What will you do? Why not take advantage of your first-hand experience with your own employer or co-worker? It's likely that someone you work with knows about marketing and brand management. If not, grab someone from the bar down the street. Take them out for a cup of coffee or a drink to pick their brain. Don't BURDEN them with your problems, but instead offer to provide value as well in the form of your knowledge. Who knows, maybe there's chemistry for a partnership.

It is your responsibility to find your mentor; they are everywhere. And you can and should have more than one.

Tip #3: Learn from your Clients and Customers:

As a shift worker serving and working with many of the same people, you likely already have a network not only of peers but also a healthy clientele. Learning from clients is easy. All you need to do is approach a client you have impressed and have a good relationship with and conduct an informal interview. Ask them everything you are curious about that a customer expects from whatever services you seek to provide. Get to the heart of the matter with as much depth as you can get away with. Repeat your informal interviews with as many customers and clients as possible.

Don't make the mistake of evaluating what the clients and customers are telling you through the lens of what you already think is true. If you do this, you will learn nothing. Remember that customers and clients are telling you about *their* experiences. Their experience is truth to them, and you must respect it as such. Don't argue, instead actively listen. You may accept or reject what they say as being relevant to you--your call--but it is imperative that you listen with an open mind and say to yourself, "This is her point of view and I need to listen to it because I'm not as smart as I think I am."

Tip #4: Analyze Available Data: Having conducted this research and have lots of notes about what you have learned from interviewing. Now what? Organize your notes, look for patterns, and write down ways to benefit from it in your own business. You will have a mishmash of data; here's how you sort through it and organize it:

- **Compile information about prospective clients:** From the research data you have acquired from your interactions with documents, relationships, surveys and interviews, you can prepare to approach your prospective clients in a smart way. The more success you get, the better the network is that you form. This is a good investment to have in your pocket once you begin to plan your own business or brand.

- **Get Organized:** I can't overstate the importance and value of getting and staying organized. I use software like Trello to organize large bodies of information and creating a visual representation of intelligence gathering has served me extremely well. More on this on my companion course at learn.jlittrell.com

- **Compile information about market trends**: From the market trends you have observed from engaging with the customers and learned about from your reading, you can do two things. One is to improve the goods or services your business offers and the processes they use to sell them. The other is to improve customer communications with the business and coming up ways to improve their satisfaction.

No good thing ever comes easy. This is especially true of success, which requires a lot of hard work. Doing research will not come easy; but the imperical or anecdotal data you gather will pay off big time.

Implementing Your Ideas

You now know that the best thing you can do right now is to serve your boss well; the second best thing you can do is learn as much as you can while still on the job. You can grow to become that irritating employee that leads the way in intensity at all aspects of the business. You have already mentally gone the next level, you have put in more effort. You have done your research.

But when you are the best person in the room, you are in the wrong room. It's time to make a change. Now that you're excellent at solving problems for your current boss, why not be your own boss and solve the problems you want to solve?

Where Do You Fit In?

Hospitality: This is a very common avenue for bartenders with a lot of creative and innovative ideas. Practical knowledge of local state and federal compliance, wage and hour laws, bar design, drafting, creative cocktail development are essential here. So, you might need to do more than just collect word-of-mouth data.

Marketing: Understanding how to connect brands with either a consumer audience, a trade audience, or both is essential in this field.

Public Relations (PR): Spirits companies hire PR companies to help them engage media (*especially* Social Media) to communicate their brand message to the world. If you have the knowledge and the knack for it, you can set yourself up for this.

Event Production: If you know how to set up and run a bar, this should be pretty easy for you. It gets tricky, however, when you get into insurance, storage, labor, and taxes. But what's tricky is worth it too.

Distribution/Sales: If you are familiar with a large range of brands and have an impressive network and/or love closing a deal, this might be the area for you. A lot of brands are not big enough to have full-time brand ambassadors, so they could definitely have a use for a person (read personal brand) who wants to work with a specific brand or category. In this area, you would engage that brand to develop recipes, host events, and angle for placements as brand support for a distributor.

Brand Management: This is also known as a market manager. Market managers are a hybrid of salespeople, brand ambassadors, and distributor managers. They work for brands and with distributors to get the word and product out. There are a large number of small brands that hire independent freelancers for this. This limits their payroll costs.

Assessing and Maximizing your Weaknesses and Strengths

After looking at the number of options you could go for, the next step is to focus on which problems you are good at solving. This section will guide you on recognizing your strengths and combining them with your brand plan.

So often the focus is on strengths, but here is the thing about weaknesses: Sometimes you can avoid them, other times you can capitalize on them. Either way, focusing on and even fixing your weaknesses alone does not cut it in the world of business.

Imagine how Guy Fieri would have reacted the first time he was told that his enthusiasm was too over-the-top or his hair looked stupid. If he had reacted to these presumed weaknesses by trying to eliminate them (or, even worse, giving up), he would not be the iconic brand he later became.

When evaluating a business opportunity, a common technique is called SWOT analysis, which stands for *Strengths, Weaknesses, Opportunities, and Threats*. Here's how you do your own SWOT analysis...

- Asking others (even your family) to tell you about your strengths and weaknesses.

- Taking an online assessment (they're everywhere on the Web)

- Check out crystalknows.com for a personality profile

- Analyze your own performance. Feedback comes from everywhere, including body language. Also, emails are good too. You can't be objective, but you can be critical. Be positive, but tough on yourself.

Analyzing your strengths is much easier. But analysis is not enough; you now need to see how you can make the most out of them. Here comes the part where you have to align your strengths with your passion.

Where do Ideas Come From?

According to Forbes magazine, there are three kinds of ideas--The Spontaneous Idea, The Insider Idea and The Deliberate Idea. If you obsess about the business, you will have a lot of Spontaneous Ideas. The Insider Idea is what dawned on you while you were interviewing somebody. The Deliberate Idea is the essential one here. Sure, you can combine all the three kinds of ideas you have accumulated. In fact, this is what you should do. This results in a Deliberate Idea. This is why it is the most crucial.

Small Businesses: The Riches are in the Niches

According to the 2012 census data, there are more than 5.73 million small businesses in the United States alone. Many small businesses start out trying to be the best at everything — that is, be the best clothing store online, or the world's greatest home decor shop. And the truth is that *it's impossible to do this*. Be the best at ONE SMALL THING, and build a service around it.

My first company started as small as it gets. I would go to industry events and see world-class cocktails served at a massive scale. In my head, I would adjust that specific recipe to hundreds or thousands of servings. I was thinking about distribution and event management and how I would reverse engineer this somewhere else. This would create some logistical puzzles to put together that really got me excited. My obsession became Critical Mass Events in 2010. All we did was events. From there it grew to hospitality consulting and then brand strategy. I found a niche, and then expanded beyond that niche.

Finding a niche does not mean you are thinking small. The hope for expansion is a good thing, but you always start small. You earn success in that niche, and THEN you think about expanding. Neil Gaiman, one of the most influential fantasy book writers, started out as a comedy writer, but now he has written across genres over decades and thrived.

Take that Niche and Add Passion

Pick out what you want to be known for and base your business on that. Remember, *it is crucial to make your strength your passion in the niche you are targeting.*

When Critical Mass was first starting out, I was obsessed with organization and problem-solving. This was an even bigger strength than my ability to assemble drinks. Even though I had been assembling drinks for a long time and loved it, it was my organizational skills that earned me larger opportunities. I started getting in large, tangled logistical messes, which I enjoyed sorting out for clients. At the time I didn't use Trello, Asana, or even Google Drive the way I rely on them now; we often had to figure things out with just pen and paper. But I did not mind that at all. When the problem aligns with your expertise, the difficulties and struggle become a motivating challenge for you to conquer.

Case Study: Colin Barceloux

When Colin Barceloux was in college, he thought textbooks cost far too much. In 2007, two years after graduating, he decided to take action and founded Bookrenter.com, a San Mateo, Californi-based business that offers textbook rentals at about a 60% discount. What began as a one-man operation created out of frustration now has 1.5 million users and 200 employees. "You just have to look at what frustrates you," Barcelous says. "There's your business idea right there."

What to Name Your Brand

Once you know what you want your business to do, it is time for you to embody the big idea in the name of your brand. We will have a discussion on using a generic name for your services to avoid limiting yourself and keeping a door open for other opportunities. You want your name to be relevant and targeted, but even just your name also works.

We have already seen that most personal brand personalities are their own brands. So their names are their brand names. If you are looking to take that approach, you cannot go wrong. Just name your brand after yourself like I eventually did. This leverages your existing reputation to service clients. Note, this is not the easier path to acquiring new customers however.

My company is called Jason Littrell, Ltd. And is a d.b.a. name which means I'm "doing business as". But my original LLC (Critical Mass Events, LLC), remains as far as taxes are concerned. I operate under a new name with a new LLC, and it was seamless. I didn't even tell the bank. I did tell my insurance agents though. The reason I did this was because ultimately, I couldn't own Critical Mass, and I would likely get a cease and desist letter eventually. So I changed my company name, got new branding, registered a new domain, and became Jason Littrell, Ltd. In the last days of 2018. The point here is that you can file for an LLC under one name, and if you decide to change it, you just simply change the branding. It doesn't have to be complicated.

Clients can write a check to me, or to Critical Mass, it doesn't make a difference. It does get more complicated when you're dealing with trademarks, partners, and many other elements, but I won't get into that here.

There has never been a more exciting time to enter into business. We have seen that from a part-time profession, people who thought themselves ordinary bartenders became business professionals. The key was doing your homework, knowing what you want, identifying your strengths, and starting out small. Excel at your niche first, then expand your business beyond the original niche. Consider a reasonably generic brand name so your services aren't pigeon-holed into a specific genre or service.

BARTENDER AS A BUSINESS

Today, more than half of Americans either own or work for a small business. It's a whole new world of economic reality. This chapter set out to establish your understanding of what your present business and what your future one can do. Keep in mind, that no matter what it is your business does, you need to be confident that you are the end and the be-all in that niche. You are different, and what you do is better. You don't have to reinvent the field, but you do have to be the leader and an original to ensure the success will follow you.

Now is the time to get out of your own head, and get started. Easier said than done...

Chapter 5

The Fears

"Of all the liars in the world, sometimes the worst are our own fears." — Rudyard Kipling

Google it, **Skype** your family, **Photoshop** that picture, **Insta** this post, **Uber** to my place. There is a whole range of brands that have become verbs, and in some cases, lifestyles. Yes, business brands have come a long way. How do you think they got their start? Do you really think that they all started off as ultra-successful? Do you really think that their founders never had doubts or second-guessed their decisions to start a business, just the same way as you might be doing? Do you think they were any different from you?

So far, we have looked at features of the hospitality business and its branding. We have also explored your options for the fields and niches, but we haven't addressed your doubts and fears of starting a brand. I understand that "putting yourself out there" is psychologically a big risk, and that the decision to do so brings forward self-doubt and even potentially catastrophic what-if scenarios (I quit my job, my business fails, my wife leaves me, I die destitute........).

This chapter will focus on your fears and worries. We will look at all of your concerns, like risking the stability of your current job, insecurity about the future, capital investment, and similar perceived difficulties. My job is to help you through that dark tunnel of self-doubt and catastrophic thinking into the light of success. If I have done my job well, this chapter will also facilitate a paradigm shift in your head about how you think about stepping into the business world. Speaking of taking a leap, let's first look at one of the biggest business successes of all time--Coca Cola, which was anything but an instant success.

The Case of Coca Cola

In its first year, 1886, Coca Cola sold 25 gallons of Coke within its own block--nine Coke bottles per day. Nine. N-I-N-E. It might as well have been the German *nein (*meaning none). Imagine standing out in the heat and cold all day as the founding pharmacist, John Pemberton, and selling only nine bottles. If your business started in this manner, I bet that you would have given up after the first year.

But John Pemberton didn't give up.

What do you think would have happened if Pemberton had given up the business based on his first-year sales? If he had done that, the world would be different today. The brand wouldn't have become a phenomenon. The world's favorite drink worth more than the combined GDPs of Bolivia, Kenya, and Bahrain wouldn't exist. They wouldn't have sold **29 billion bottles** in 2017. (That's enough for each person in London to drink 206 bottles of Coca-Cola in a single day for the whole year.) Today, around 1.9 billion servings of Coca Cola are consumed every day in the world.

Case Study: Jason Littrell

At my old job at Death & Co, I was treated as "the new guy" for the entire two, and a half years I was there. I loved it because I was always felt like the student of the newest and oldest bartenders alike. I learned everything I possibly could. Eventually, I built a business adapting those skills to large-format cocktails, and, when I was good enough, I ultimately took on marketing and strategy for spirits and hospitality brands, not as gigs, but as services.

I loved making cocktails, and I loved learning about new ways of constructing cocktails. But what I lacked was inventiveness. I wasn't making my own original recipes, like the people around me were doing. I was reasonably good at making drinks--my strength was somewhat useful there--but it still wasn't the X factor that would propel me to where I wanted to see myself. I came to realize that my strengths in marketing and strategy were uniquely strong, and so I started thinking about putting myself out there in a different way. This required confidence, and a healthy appetite for constructive failure.

Excuses: Tell Me Why You Can't Become a Business

One universal trait of human nature is that we always have plenty of excuses NOT to do the things we don't want to do. It takes tremendous energy to take that first step into something scary. It's much easier to stay the same, which takes no energy.

The step we want to take may be for our own good, but it requires us to disrupt the order of our entire current existence. It means to stop being stuck and taking that leap to get on the other side. It means to stop complaining and start doing. Fear generates so many creative excuses. Excuses block our motivation and boost our confidence for NOT pursuing the things that are good for us.

Make a list of the reasons you should not go from bartender to business.

I'll bet you will come up with at least 100.

Now, let's get real and take a look at some facts. You have been working as a bartender for awhile. Your experience and network qualify to start a business. Why? Because you are now a problem solver for potential clients, which makes you valuable.

The excuses that you are so easily generating right now come from that superior organ, the brain. And they are completely understandable. Don't think by any means that I am invalidating your excuses for why you cannot start your own business. But this book is here to help you eliminate those doubts and excuses. As Dr. Robert Anthony said, *"Forget about all the reasons why something may not work. You only need to find one good reason why it will."*

Remember Guy and Charles.

Banishing Excuses

We are going to look at some of the reasons why you (and your brain) think this prospect will not work. These reasons will help you understand why you are unwilling to budge in the direction of starting a business. Here are five of them:

- Fear of leaving behind the stability of your current job.

- Insufficient capital for investment.

- Fear about no longer being able to see what the future holds.

- Concerns that you are inexperienced at managing a business.

- You're just not ready.

Most excuses fall into one of these categories, so let's look at these in more detail.

Fear of leaving behind the stability of your current job: Congratulations, you have a job. You are now one of the 96% of the Americans who have jobs. Still want to congratulate yourself? On the other hand, if you are a business owner, you are among an elite 13% of Americans.

Having a job is definitely a good thing; a job is a source of stability and order. You are earning something every month and supporting your family. Unfortunately, having a job is stability, not necessarily security.

The idea of starting a business is immediately associated with the idea of letting go of a job. That is only partly true. You can expand your business gradually while you are still working. When your business starts doing better for you than your "real job," then you quit your job. It's that simple. You do not have to dive into the swimming pool of business right away; you can dip your toes in first and slowly inch your way into the water.

What you need is a strategic plan for balancing your work and your business. We'll explore that in detail later.

Having Your Cake and Eating it Too

Have you ever had a delicious chocolate cake all to yourself to eat? If yes, reminisce fondly; if not, use your imagination! How did you finish it? You ate one (two for me please), stored it in the fridge and finished eating the rest gradually, right? The same concept applies to your job and your business.

You don't have to eat the whole cake at once! The best part about starting a business is that you start small. You can eat the cake by the slice while you keep going about your stable life. Just progress gradually by the chunk. Eventually, you will have your cake and will eat it too.

Insufficient Capital for Investment: The thoughts of capital worry you a lot because you have believed in a myth. Starting a business does NOT require a lot of money. You do not need much more than a computer, and an intense drive for self-determination. It *does* take a lot of **reinvestment,** though. Do you have a small desk or a kitchen table? Perfect. You do not need even need an office. I get some of my best work done in bed. For me, the biggest differentiator is DISTRACTION. According to research, 69% of U.S. based entrepreneurs start their businesses at home. Elon Musk was one of those who started his entrepreneurial project from his home. Today, his net worth is around $22 billion.

Capital is useful, but it's also a limitation. Not having it teaches you to operate lean. A business startup does not need capital as badly as it needs a plan. Your plan should be far-sighted enough so that when you finally decide to quit your job, you have as much money saved as your business startup will require. Re-prioritize your spending. Do your research and come up with a plan according to your jurisdiction and market, and come up with a safe figure you think you can invest in your business. My initial investment in my business was about $350.

There are also other options such as small business loans, crowdfunding, or simply asking friends and family to invest in you, but I wouldn't recommend going into debt, unless you know exactly how it's going to be paid back with a meaningful return. If you are determined, if you believe in yourself and your vision, money will not be your problem. It is out there. You just have to find it. Real entrepreneurs don't let money stand in the way.

Fear about no longer being able to see what the future holds: "Vision" is an intuitive prediction. What is your vision? If you are afraid of the future, and fear failure, your vision is blurred. The truth is, failure is an essential element of success. It's not something to be afraid of, it's something that adds more value to you in the form of experience. Our imaginations tend to be much more vivid than our realities.

Imagine yourself in ten, fifteen or twenty years from now. Imagine the best that could come out of these years. What does success look like? If you have or would like to have a spouse or kids, what will their lifestyle be like? What kind of education will they have? What will your house look like? Compare your current situation with your vision and see how realistic it is for you to achieve the best. Then, reverse engineer that vision. Are you on the path to that life with your current job and situation?

With your own business, you can be. What is the worse that could happen with starting small? Will you lose your capital investment? Your reinvestment? You will still not go bankrupt most likely. You may need some lean months or years, but unless you're going to some crazy high-stakes operation (like say a pilot, or a surgeon), you can't really do that much harm to yourself or to others. If you're really worried, that's what insurance is for.

To me, regret is a far more powerful motivation. Imagine looking back and saying to yourself, why didn't I take the leap back then? If you start your business now, your business has lots of years to grow thrive. How old will you be in 20 years if you start your own business? How old will you be in the same 20 years if you never started it?

Concerns about your ability to manage a business: In India, the Indian Institutes of Technology (IITs) are considered highly prestigious. In fact, these Institutes are so highly regarded that a graduate from an IIT can expect to be immediately hired without a need to give any U.S. based test or educational investment. But here is a fun fact: The CEO of Google, Sundar Pichai, a South Indian, did not study from an IIT. Today, his net worth is $600 million.

Passion is much more important than qualifications. With your passion, you will soak up every detail about working the business. Right now you need to only capitalize on the research you have done and the skills you have acquired. Make use of mentoring and one day you will be mentoring others. You do not need a flashy degree (or any degree) from an eminent (or otherwise) college. You just need some sense of how things work and a willingness to step up. The single best way to gain experience in running a business is by starting one.

You're Just Not Ready. I'm going to present to you two scenarios. If you think the following things have happened to you, raise your hands.

☐

ave you ever waited to text a person "at the right time" but the right time never came, and it got too late anyway?

☐

id you ever get a good opportunity that you squandered just because you thought you are not ready?

I have. And, in all likelihood, so have you. Procrastination is just another one of those universal human traits. Sometimes, you keep waiting for an opportunity to knock when you should have broken the door down yourself. In truth, the "I'm not ready" excuse is a myth. You are saying that you are too lazy and/or too fearful to try something new. You may think you are not ready for business because you are focusing on one or more of the negative things in your life. Instead of focusing on your values according to who you ARE or what you HAVE, you are focusing on who you AREN'T and what you don't HAVE. It could be one of the things mentioned above, such as experience or qualifications. It could also be you comparing yourself with other business owners and crossing out the skills you don't have. Don't do that. You're not like them. You're You.

You may say to yourself, "I'll do it after just one more year," "I'll do it after my kid is born," "I'll do it after my son graduates" until it eventually becomes "I'll do it after I retire." Imagine your regret then. The only time that matters is now, and the only time you are ready is when you think and believe that you are ready.

Remember that you are the best (and only) person that can do what YOU do. Don't try to imitate other people or companies.

Starting a Business is Easy. Staying in Business Is Hard.

Any idiot can start a business – look at me, I've done it. However, it's not the starting of the business but staying in business that is the difficult thing to do.

BARTENDER AS A BUSINESS

Starting a business in today's world is like having a treadmill. You can buy one, have it delivered straight to your house. Then you have to plug it in. This is how you get into shape, right? No, you have to run ON the machine.

When I first started out, I had no idea what I was doing. I learned about it in the process of starting my company. Almost a decade later, I'm still figuring it out. For me, that's the fun part. I won't lie, It's not easy. But what you've been developing over the last several years while grinding out shifts, learning efficiencies, speaking the language, and putting the work in, qualifies you to open your own shop (either literally or figuratively). Down the road, I used the techniques that I had learned to adapt and expand into other service offerings using the same principles, the same *mise*. And I can tell you, with all the passion and excitement in these years, it has been more fun and lucrative than working a job because I know it's limitless, and I started as the CEO. I will never be an employee again.

Being an entrepreneur, even for a short time, is an extremely valuable resource for an employer. Entrepreneurs know how to solve problems. Entrepreneurs don't ask "Why," they ask "How." Thus, elevating yourself to this position automatically strengthens your position. Who wouldn't want someone like that on their team?

In this chapter, we have seen that the biggest limitation to starting a business is your own fear and excuses. We looked at how to tackle that fear and those excuses. I also made the case that there really isn't a lot of risk involved in a business startup. If the shit hits the fan, all you lost was the cost of this book. If you build it, they will hire you.

Now, let's do this thing!

PART 2

MAKING IT HAPPEN

Chapter 6

The Cornerstone

"It was October 2010, and I was lying in bed thinking about the future, and what I wanted. I was headstrong, impatient, and very ambitious. I didn't know what I was going to do, but I knew that what I was doing wasn't exactly sustainable. I started doing google searches about starting a business. I had no idea what I was getting in to."

In Chapter 5, we discussed how you can prepare yourself for making the huge leap of starting a business, ESPECIALLY while you're still working another job. We discussed how to think about and organize your capital investment, how to manage your fears and so on. What comes after you get over your fears and anxieties and decide to start out?

As with that first bartending job, half the work was getting the job, and half the work was doing the job. Similarly, in the entrepreneurial world, half the job is starting the business, and the rest is putting in the work for your business.

In this chapter, we will look at big questions such as picking a business name, creating a brand image, using the internet as a tool, setting up the infrastructure of your brand and going through some dos and don'ts. At the end of this chapter, you will gain a clearer understanding of your next set of steps and options.

Brand Identity

"Brand identity is what a brand stands for and how it is perceived in the world," said Denny Sanders. "It's the words, thoughts, and images that come to mind when the consumer engages with the brand in some way – and how it makes the consumer feel."

In other words, brand identity is the voice you give to your product or service.

There are plenty of brands that have developed incredible brand identities. Think of **Adobe** – the company defined by its devotion to art and creativity.

For your brand building, you have to think of the maxim inscribed in the Temple of Apollo: *"Know thyself."* It holds more weight than you might think. To establish a voice for your brand, be aware of yourself and your intentions. The way consumers identify with brands is not random; it is a rational process foreseen by the brands' owners.

What will your brand say?

Brand Image

The difference between the brand identity and brand image is the same as the difference between what you would say to someone and what they hear. What you launch is not necessarily what lands. Brand Image is what lands.

You think of pricey innovations and Steve Jobs when you imagine **Apple**; you think of timed pictures and videos when you think of **Snapchat**. Similarly, you can think of other brands and tell me what sensations or thoughts arise in you when you think of them.

The customer is not necessarily buying a product or service. They are buying the image associated with that product or service. Have you ever received an **Amazon Prime** package in the mail? What was inside it? A mobile phone? A skateboard? A box of crayons? Whatever it was, your ultimate product had an inescapable, unavoidable link with **Amazon Prime** service. You purchased not only the product; you also purchased a subscription to the source of the service.

Companies try to make the brand image unique, positive and instantly recognizable by setting up their infrastructure efficiently and intelligently. You can also strengthen your brand image through packaging, advertising, publicizing through word of mouth and other promotional tools.

Case Study: Ugly Drinks Inc

Ugly Drinks Inc aims to provide a healthy alternative to all sugary soft drinks that consumers currently drink. This was their brand identity, what their voice was, what they wished to be known for. But how were they perceived?

The name of the brand created a negative image in the minds of its customers. The poor name choice was only made worse by the previous look of the company, which focused on a complete clunky typeface displayed at a weird angle. The Brand Identity failed to convey the image the company intended.

The infrastructure of a Brand

Have you ever thought about the evolution of a brand? How does a brand evolve?

At first, there is an **idea of a brand**, a vague idea of the product's attributes. Then we have **brand as actions**, or all the great ideas used to build the brand. In the end, you have the **brand as network**, or the culmination of all the assets and networks that the brand owns.

Let's look at what some of the brands have accomplished as their end result of becoming a network:

Starbucks created a coffee culture. ***Uber*** defined a new commute lifestyle. ***Warby Parker*** made eyewear convenient, seasonal, and affordable.

How?

These brands not only executed better ideas, but they also built a better infrastructure envisioning the evolution of their brand. This was not an accident; it was done by design.

Brands are usually incentivized to standardize. This means they are trying to sell repeatable blocks of time and space. They build their brand experience around existing user behavior, which they try to conform to through their brand's delivery and actions. But you don't want to do this. You want to ensure that what you are setting up is **unique**, THEN you can systemize (not standardize).

Great brands think about the desired behavior, not existing behavior. They understand what people would like to do, even when people don't know it themselves. Modern brands enable new behaviors and create rituals based upon either delivering unique experiences or delivering experiences that feel to be new. They don't simply fit into a customer's existing day; they make that day better.

Building an excellent business infrastructure right when you are starting out will save you an enormous amount of time and money down the road. In addition, it will help you understand your brand at every step of the way. You will think about your brand continuously, and you will get to know it better. Your vision will be clearer, your mission statement more defined, and your strategies more reflexive.

Besides the basic hospitality skills that you have, you will need a deeper understanding of how things work. Preparing and serving food and beverage, making small talk with your customers, managing hotel accommodations--these are not enough. You need to be a jack-of-all-trades in the industry, as well as well-aligned with your research about branding and business. As a bartender, mixologist, or anyone in the hospitality industry, you need to understand something about architecture, legal and compliance, IT, marketing, social media, human resources management, accounting, finance, statistics, revenue management, etc. Your brand will test your knowledge in all these areas. In the end, these will become vital when you put your business in place using the right tools.

Just like *mise en place*, have a place to put your expenses, your taxes, your dollars, and your ideas. There are a million different setups for a micro business. I will show you what you need to get started.

First, Decide on a Business Name

We have discussed the importance of your business name briefly earlier on. It is now time for a callback and further discussion.

Naming your business or brand is a lot like laying the cornerstone of a building. Once it is in place, it supports the entire foundation and structure. If it is not strong, the rest of the building tilts, and the misalignment becomes amplified. So the key is to set up strong foundations through a brand name that fully supports what your brand stands for.

Having had some general experience in naming and branding, I've witnessed the good, the bad and the really really bad. My best advice for you would be to go generic, but make your brand easily distinguishable from other brand names.

The right name can make your brand a buzzword. Your brand name could become a verb. The wrong one can confuse and disorient. Ideally, your brand name should convey the expertise, value, and uniqueness of the product or service you have developed.

I recommend going generic. This is because I believe that the best names are abstract and general, like a blank slate upon which you create an image. Consider the brand name *Tesla*. If you know your history, the first thing that comes to your is the scientist Nikola Tesla and perhaps his incredible advances in our understanding of electricity. Your mind instantly associates it with some techy stuff, and this helps the Tesla brand a lot. It does not specify or restrict what the company can be, yet it has established the name as an automotive and energy company.

Others think names should be informative, so customers know immediately what your business is. Consider the brand *Italiatour*. You immediately get a sense of what the brand is about. The name communicates, without being an actual word in the dictionary, that the company sells package tours to Italy. If it did not do that, the customer would feel cheated. Similarly, consider *NameLab*. It is the name of a brand naming service. They help you come up with a brand name when you get stuck. I personally don't recommend hiring other people for your own brand name unless you have serious financial backing. You owe it to your brand the basic creativity to name it, just as you would name your child. Talk to people, come up with a ton of bad ideas. This will diversify your input, thus consodating your output.

To gain inspiration, walk or drive around the town and think about the brand names that pop up before you on billboards and advertisements. Think about names such as **Monster.com**, **eBay**, **Marriott Hotels**, and think about their appeal. Then, write down the ideas that come from your own name, especially the bad ones. Your brain will associate them and keep throwing you better ones.

What do you do after you've narrowed the field to four or five names that are memorable and expressive? You simply refine them further to the two or three best ones. Then you go over your brand manifesto, your ideas, services, strategies, etc. and revisit the names. Inspiration will ultimately strike.

Remember that people and companies invest in other people way more than they invest in a faceless brand. This does not mean that you take the brand name lightly; rather, it means that you should not spend all your time coming up with the brand name. Choose a name and then move on. YOU are the business. We have already discussed the importance of personality and identity through figures such as Emeril Lagasse and Charles Joly. Similarly, you are the face and persona of your brand. Make sure your identity is engaged in your brand.

Tools Related to Brand Imaging

I highly recommend using **DesignCrowd** to set up your Brand Image. It's an investment, but for me it was worth it! DesignCrowd does it all--logos, business cards, T-shirts, website designs, cartoon character design, and even envelope design. Your logo is just as important as your brand name. It complements it and aligns your brand image accordingly.

As in a letter, your e-mail signature is a critical conveyor of your brand. The signature often contains the sender's name, contact information, email address, a website URL, etc. **Emailsignaturerescue**'s intuitive software provides you with a live editor and all the tools you will need to customize email signatures for your brand, from anywhere, at any time. It will incorporate your logo and even appealing attachments such as pictures or gifs. It helps you select from over 200,000 social icons in various styles, colors, and sizes, then link them directly to your social media pages. Along with this, there is also Google Analytics tracking available to any link, include disclaimers, privacy text, green messages, etc.

It's like they say, leaving a lasting impression is hard. I say, doing it at the end of an email is even harder. Which is why I let the software do it for me.

Second, Build a Website

You've chosen a name and are ready to move on. Now you need a Website. This guide is hardly exhaustive, but the best resource I've found to learn how to build a website is YouTube. Everything knowable is on YouTube. Broadly speaking, keep your site simple, short, and communicate everything a client needs to know about you and your business in about 10 seconds. A single page is more than sufficient for most freelancers' needs. Also, always have a call to action button "Book a call" or "Buy Now."

Before you start building a website, you'll need a domain. You can get this through your host, or by going to my favorite

namecheap.com. This is effectively a piece of real estate, and an interesting side hustle is to buy domains only to sell them. The resale value is only limited by what a customer is willing to pay. I often buy domains I think might be valuable, and list them for sale. This is about a $9 investment. Imagine what a derivative domain name would be worth to a billion-dollar company?

You'll also need hosting. With Squarespace and Wix, you don't have to worry about this, but for Wordpress, you'll need a host. I use **Hostwinds**, but another good host is **Blue Host.** Your host is the offsite computer (server) that stores all the information from your website. These are on 24/7/365, and are often backed up with redundant servers in different physical locations, constantly updated and manicured by a small army of data scientists who protect your data.

Choosing a website builder (also known as a Content Mangement System or CMS) is hard because there are so many options to choose from. It's like being at an amusement park with only one pass to any ride, trying to decide which ride to go on. Everything looks so exciting, and it's easy to feel overwhelmed. In this section, I will help you decide by taking a closer look at Wix, Squarespace, and WordPress, all widely-used and extremely powerful. A common misconception is that you need to know how to code. You don't. Additionally, this skill is incredibly high in demand, so mastering just this one skill could be the focus of your business if you wanted.

Wix (wix.com): Wix is fun for all ages, and the easiest builder to use. You never feel lost when building a Wix website because it's so intuitive. According to several reviews, Wix is the best *overall* website builder on the market. It's the complete package: great value, easy to use, and backed by superb customer support.

It has its cons, though. Once you settle on a theme, it sticks with you for life. You cannot switch themes after publishing. Its drag-and-drop design makes it easy to reshape your website, but there are so many options to choose from. This choice can feel overwhelming.

Squarespace (squarespace.com): Squarespace is like Wix's more fashionable sibling. It is the leader in design. It has beautifully crafted templates suited to any industry. Because it is best for creative industries, it is perfect for the hospitality businesses. With such beauty, however, comes a steeper learning curve.

Squarespace is relatively difficult to use at first. However, as you practice, play with it, and become more proficient, you will find that you are able to create a magical website. Squarespace is relatively expensive compared to Wix.

Wordpress.com: WordPress is the classical option that powers about 60% of internet websites. It has a great publishing appeal. However, Wordpress is for tech-savvy users (or users who don't mind a steep learning curve) who want total freedom in customization, or for people willing to spend hours learning about coding and hosting.

Now, this can be both a good thing and a bad thing. If you have the programmer's hand and eye, you can make your website sing and do all kinds of widely customizable things. Your Website will be limited only by your own skill level. I've always used Wordpress for my sites, but I don't know how to code. I rely on the incredible array of free and paid templates out there and

You can try taking a free run at each of the three website builders, and you're your choice through trial and error method. But remember--like deciding on a brand name--you don't want building the website itself to become your life's work. Build a Website and then move on.

Third, Set Up Checklists

For a personal business startup, we have already briefly discussed the significance of LLCs, S-Corp, and so on. It is up to you to decide whether you need insurance at this stage and what the impact on your taxes will be.

To organize your business, whether it be prior to you quitting your job or after, I suggest you to use checklists to streamline your work. Documenting your process is essential to scaling your business. Checklists are how they fly planes and how they perform surgeries. Hospitals and airports alike make use of Web-based list-making applications to organize and track their work. Research on and get used to checklists. It will improve your productivity.

I use **Trello** to keep monster checklists under control. My days and sometimes even weeks are organized because I have set everything up on the application. All assignments and assignment tracking are present on the many virtual cards and lists. I never have to burden my mind with trying to remember, and so I don't have to do the same work twice. With this kan ban methodology, I am able to identify and prioritize tasks so I'm only working on what is most important at any particular time.

Your Homework: Read The E-Myth

Check out the book **The EMyth**, which offers business and executive coaching to business owners. None of my suggestions are a reasonable replacement for having a good lawyer and a good accountant or bookkeeper, but you don't know what you don't know. It's far cheaper to pay attorney fees than it is to A) go to law school, or B) get locked into a bad deal. No deal is better than a bad deal.

This chapter intended to boost your entrepreneurial IQ after you decided to build a business. Like they say, well begun is half done. Yet, it is still only half done.

Having all the tools and expecting a product to pop out is a lot like buying a movie camera and expecting a movie to come out. It just doesn't work out like that. You still have to do the work.

There will be decisions you have to make and unmake. Do as much research as you can, add on to your research, and decide accordingly. Don't worry if it doesn't work out; the worst-case scenario is that you are stuck with it for awhile. After that, you fail, and you may either return to your job or to your business, trying to fail better.

After having seen about starting up, the next chapter will focus on how you can sell your skills to other people.

Chapter 7

Letting Your Brand Tell Your Story

"The best brands are built on great stories."

We are now transitioning from the mechanical to the artistic. There is no better art than the art of good storytelling. Stories, and the ability to tell them, are critically important components of branding and I will show you why. It may sound odd, unheard-of, and unconventional, but your ability to tell a story (your story!) will determine how well you differentiate your brand. This chapter will help you find and tell your brand story. Your story will lay the foundation of your brand and also allow you to expand in the future. A good success story can build your brand, make it famous via word of mouth, and even turn your brand into a verb.

Why Does a Brand Have to Tell a Story?

Think about the beginning of Judeo-Christian history. What did we have first? The story of Adam and Eve and the apple, of course! It has been thousands of years, and the world has not forgotten it. And every culture on earth has a similar origin story. Why? Because it resonates with us timelessly.

What if your brand could tell a story that stays with your customers for a really long time?

Just because we tell a story, that doesn't automatically mean that our story is interesting. Close your eyes and try to imagine how many revolutionary and visionary brands there are out there that go unnoticed. Why is that? Because their stories weren't interesting.

Many brands trap themselves into a "quantity over quality" paradigm, forsaking compelling storytelling for product-centric content. This approach emphasizes product movement (sales) over storytelling. It is no surprise that this approach does not really move the needle because it doesn't ensnare the customer with its stories. (Do you swoon when you hear the brand name Bostitch Stapler? I didn't think so.) Put the marketing advantage on your side (on the side of storytelling), and you will find that there is no better way to attract your audience than by evoking their emotions.

As a business starter--and more so as a service or hospitality business starter--you may not have thought about the link between brands and stories. In reality, brand storytelling is everywhere, and it is not going anywhere. In an era when people are tired of being talked at and sold to, people crave genuine connections with brands. This is what a story gives, a *connection*.

We have seen an explosion in brand content, but how much of it actually resonates? How do you make your brand story matter? We will tackle these questions, but for now, let's focus on defining what a brand story is.

What is a Brand Story?

The question is, what is a brand story? The answer is, it's how Starbucks created a whole new coffee category and rose above its rivals. That answer is the reason why so many people drive miles out of their way, passing Dunkin Donuts and 7 Eleven, to pay three times more for a cup of coffee every morning.

A brand story provides the narrative that illuminates your company's creation story, and expresses how that narrative still pushes its mission today. It is not unlike what happens when your favorite books and movie characters become a part of you. When one asks, "What is your favorite story (or character) of all time?," you very likely have an answer ready. If you can craft a compelling brand story, your audience will similarly remember who you are and what your brand is all about. They will develop empathy for you, talk and tweet about you, and, ultimately, care about you.

However, a brand story is more than content and a narrative. In reality, the story goes beyond what we write up in Website copy, the text we generate for a brochure or the presentation we use to pitch to investors or customers. A brand story is not just a catchy tagline that's pasted on a billboard to attract attention for a week or two. Your story is not just what you tell people; it's also what they believe about you based on the signals your brand sends. The story is a complete picture made up of facts, feelings, and interpretations. You do more than tell your story; you embody it.

Every action you take, each element of your business or brand, from the colors and texture of your packaging and business cards to the staff you hire, aligns with your brand story. You live your brand story even after you have told it and published it. Every element of your storytelling should reflect the truth about your brand. If your story does not accurately depict your brand, your audience will detect that and your brand will lose its allure.

If you want to build a successful, sustainable business and a brand that will garner loyalty, you have to start with your story. I am well aware that you might be saying to yourself, "he's overstating the poetics of this thing……." No. I'm not.

The Importance of a Brand Story

Here is a secret that many business starters do not know: all the big brands build themselves on so much more than the utility and specifications of their products.

Your product is only part of the story. Your customer's relationship with your brand will begin before they actually purchase your product at all.

A study found that people spend more money on everything from hotel rooms to paintings when products or services pair themselves with a story. When you go to a museum, you are not just there for the artifacts. You are there to learn about the stories behind them. The same is true for brands. The world may appear materialistic, but people undeniably crave connections, even if it is to objects and ideas. In the words of Ilya Verdashko, "Stories move not only people, but they also move product."

Why do you suppose that charities show you pictures of homeless animals or hungry children in their commercials in order to get you to contribute? Because they want you to connect with the story, of course. A study by a neuro-economist found that a character-driven story causes people to donate 56% more money to charity. This was because there is a correlation between how stories and how they shape our brains. They tie strangers together and move us to be more empathetic and generous. This is why, rather than go simply for a set of facts, good brands try to tie their products with compelling stories. This is how more of the customer's brain is engaged, and products are remembered more acutely.

In spite of this, according to a survey, only 17% of marketers were found to be using storytelling in their content. This is in spite of the fact that, of the most successful content marketers (we are talking the 2% of biggest business conglomerates here), 83% reported that storytelling plays a significant role in their content marketing.

Still don't believe me? Just watch one episode of Shark Tank, which is all about brand storytelling, and you will see very clearly what I am talking about.

Incorporate storytelling in your marketing and brand content, and the results will amaze you. The question springs up, though. How do you write a brand story? Keep reading...

Brand Storytelling Essentials

Telling a good brand story comes down to crafting a strong narrative that hooks people. For brands, there are many creative ways to create that connection. Out of all your skills, the most important one you have is your imagination and how wild you are willing to run with it. Before we get into too much detail about brand storytelling, here are three essentials that you need to know:

Brand storytelling Essential #1:
Make your brand the hero of your story. Think of security software that protects a small business from identity theft. Whatever the problem is, your brand is the solution.

Brand Storytelling Essential #2:
Make your brand part of the customer's story. A brand's comfy shoes can help their customers cross the finish line first. Similarly, a consultant's help will spare you the labor pain of a specialty, and either create more, or save you money. Invite the customer to ponder these questions: What would my life look like if I hire this consultant? What would my life look like if I DIDN'T hire this consultant?

Brand Storytelling Essential #3: **Tell stories about your brand's people, values, origin, and philosophy.**

Jason Littrell

How to Write a Brand Story

A 2014 study examined popular Super Bowl ads and found that the most popular ads weren't those that were the silliest, most outrageous, or most hilarious. The most popular ads were the ones that followed a familiar dramatic arc. Let's head back to Creative Writing 101 and take a look at Gustav Freytag's Pyramid. Freytag's Pyramid is a diagram of dramatic structure outlining the seven key steps in successful storytelling: exposition, inciting incident, rising action, climax, falling action, resolution, and denouement.

A great brand story crafts a narrative that follows that arc—and ends with a resolution (or solution—which is, ideally, your product or service). For starters, and to get your juices flowing, think of a story that will take your readers or viewers on a journey.

Here are four common themes for journey stories: may include a problem/solution, before/after, tutorials, or underdog story. Some of the most common include:

Type of Journey Story	Product/Approach
Present problem, present solution	Snickers ("You're not YOU when you're hungry.")
Describe before, describe after	What you're like before you drink Red Bull, and what you're like after you drink Red Bull.
Provide a tutorial	Facebook and Snapchat
Tell an underdog Story	How a small mom-and-pop disrupted an entire industry.

Some Questions to Ask Yourself about your Story

Not every story will capture people's attention, and no story will capture everyone's attention. But every piece of content you put out into the universe should serve one purpose and one purpose only for the people who will consume it-- telling your story.

I encourage you to brainstorm with yourself or among your friends and peers about what your story is. Here are a few questions in order to get your creative juices flowing:

- Why do I want to tell this story?
- What's my unique angle?
- What value will this provide to my audience?
- What should my audience take away from this?

Following these, you can ask the following "is it" questions:

- Is it meaningful?
- Is it personal?
- Is it emotional?
- Is it simple?
- Is it authentic?

I recommend that you get a sample audience (a group that consists of members of the population you hope to reach) together to read and verify your story before you release it to the wider audience:

At this point, the process may sound very tedious to you. The truth is that it is. The audience needs to know how your brand improves their life. They need to have a reason why they should take the time to invest in you. Remember: If there is no place for the customer in your story, there's no reason for them to pay attention to it. A strong brand story is all about stimulating emotion and empathy. It's not just about what you do but how you affect people and bring a change into their lives.

The Role of Conflict in Storytelling

Read the following story and see if it resonates with you:

A girl wearing a red-hooded cloak is strolling through the woods to give her sick grandma some much-needed food and TLC. She passes by a wolf on her route. They exchange a slightly awkward soft smile-nod combination that random colleagues use to greet each other with as they pass in the hallway. She makes it to her grandma's house without a scratch. They eat lunch and play a game of Clue together. Grandma wins by deducing that Colonel Mustard killed Mr. Boddy in the Billiard Room with the candlestick -- what a shocker! The End.

So, what did you think? Did this story keep you on the edge of your seat? Or does it feel... off? For some reason, it doesn't work, right? That's because there's no conflict. Despite the intense game of Clue at the end, there's nothing at stake. There's no tension. The wolf didn't try to eat the girl.

126

He didn't even go to Grandma's house. He barely acknowledged Little Red Riding Hood.

At their core, stories are about overcoming adversity. If there's no conflict present, there's no drama or emotional journey that people can relate to. There is no Hamlet's father's death; there is no evil queen who makes Snow White run away into the forest. If your story has no drama or emotional journey, it will fail to hold anyone's attention – let alone resonate with and inspire them.

Unfortunately, in the business world, brands tend to be reluctant to reveal any adversity or conflict they have faced. They believe that spinning a rosy, blemish-free story about how their company only experiences exponential growth will convince people they're the industry's best-in-class solution. Any adversity or conflict during their company's history will expose their imperfections, deterring potential customers from buying their product.

This is unrealistic and utopian. The real world is not like that.

In reality, nothing is perfect. Everything, including companies (especially companies), have flaws. Plus, people don't relate to perfection. They relate to the emotional journey of experiencing adversity, struggling through it, and, ultimately, overcoming it. Because, in a nutshell, that's the story of life.

Conflict is key to telling compelling stories, and it follows with a resolution. So be transparent about the adversity your company has faced, own it, and show your resolve for doing away with it. The more honest you are about your shortcomings, and the more efficient your solution, the stronger the appeal of your story will be to your customers. This is a great opening social media strategy for your consulting business. Share the journey.

Status Quo, Conflict and Resolution

After so many theoretical discussions, I think it is about time we get more practical. Let us look at some examples of storytelling and some case studies to deepen your understanding.

Case Study #1: Unthinkable Media

Unthinkable Media is a creative agency that produces original, narrative-driven podcasts for B2B brands. its mission is to create refreshing, entertaining shows for clients that can keep people's attention, not just gain it.

Status Quo: As makers and marketers, we want our audience's attention, and so for years, we focused our efforts on gaining and sustaining it.

Conflict: But today, thanks to multiple screens, ubiquitous and instantly accessible content, and endless choice in nearly every competitive niche, the buyer now has total control. They only choose the experiences they genuinely enjoy. It is no longer enough for us to simply gain our audience's attention.

Resolution: We need to hold our audience's attention. This is our new mandate as makers and marketers. We need to shift our focus from impressions and traffic to subscribers and the community. Everything we are trying to achieve becomes possible and gets easier when our audience spends minutes or even hours with us, not seconds. Don't just gain attention. Hold it.

Case Study #2: Grado Labs

Grado Labs is a third-generation, family-owned headphone and cartridge company. They don't believe in advertising, have operated in the same building for over a century, and even make their headphones by hand. So why do they operate like this when huge brands like Beats by Dre, Sony, and Bose have celebrity endorsers and mass-produce their headphones?

Status Quo: Music is an essential part of the human experience. Without it, life just isn't as colorful and exciting. And we believe quality headphones amplify the pleasant, emotional experience of listening to music.

Conflict: In a market where every headphone brand has an enormous advertising budget, state-of-the-art facilities, and high-tech machines that can churn out as much product as they want, all of which we don't have, why do we choose not to conform?

Resolution: Sound comes first. We're craft-driven creators, meaning we prioritize producing the best product over generating the most hype. By creating a better pair of headphones at the expense of publicity and growth, we can serve our customers better and foster a fervent passion for our product.

Case Study #3: Drift

Drift is a conversational marketing platform that helps businesses connect with prospects through genuine, empathetic conversations and interactions. In 2016, they shocked the content marketing world by scrapping arguably the most

reliable lead generator from their website —
forms. Even though they were initially anxious
about getting rid of a lead generation machine,
they knew un-gating every piece of content on
their website would allow them to align with their
mission. It would put their customers first, and
offer as much value as possible, which would
produce better long-term results.

Status Quo: The crux of content marketing is
treating people like humans. So, we've done what
most other companies have done: created content
that aims to help and educate our customers. And
in exchange for adding value to their lives,
customers are likely to return the favor with their
attention, trust, and action.

Conflict: But as much as we preach about putting
the customer first, we don't practice it. Instead of
offering the most value we possibly can, we make
people give us their contact information in
exchange for the very thing we promise is free.
Then, with their contact information, we email and
call them until they either unsubscribe or
eventually buy. No one actually enjoys filling out
forms, becoming a lead, and getting nurtured. Our
ulterior motive is crystal clear. So are we actually
being customer-centric?

Resolution: Let's get rid of all our forms. If we really
want to practice what we preach — putting our

customers first and providing a more human and empathetic marketing experience — we should offer all of our content for free, with no strings attached.

In all three cases, the company considered the pros and cons of telling the story (i.e., handling the conflict) in a different way. What is the potential conflict in your brand and how will you resolve it?

If your brand does not have a story, you are just another commodity; a replaceable cog in the consumption machine. You have no way to differentiate your brand or your business. Creating a brand story is not simply about standing out and getting noticed. It is about building something that people care about and want to buy into. It adds to the life story of people's lives. If you have a story that makes people believe (and delivers) that your product could change people's lives, your brand has achieved it. This comes from thinking beyond the utility and functionality of products and services, and striving for the creation of loyalty and meaningful bonds with your customers.

In today's world, everyone is dealing with content shock. There are a million brands vying for attention, hopping on whatever hip bandwagon their competitors are on. That's why brands are all suddenly churning out infographics or interactives – and get disappointed when they don't "hit" the way they had hoped. Why? Because many brands focus too much on what they want to create and not how they can make people actually care about it.

Now that you have a story to tell, let's talk about how to promote that story.

Chapter 8

Promoting Your Brand

Okay, you've done everything I've asked you to do in previous chapters, and you have set your story up. That is incredible! But you are still only halfway there. After all, what is a story without somebody to enjoy it? In this chapter, we are going to talk about how to push your story and brand out into the world. Remember when we talked about marketing and promoting in Chapter One? Those are the basics. We are now moving to the next level because you're ready for it.

Let us first review what we have already learned about marketing.

We previously talked about marketing your service by captivating your customer's psyche. We talked about personalization and trust, and how these are interconnected and inseparable. You now know that marketing is more than just advertising and publicity; it is about scanning the market to identify your target customers and appeal to their particular needs. Your job is simply to meet those needs. We also explored the 7-38-55% rule and the importance of marketing tools to promote your product.

Networking is another critical idea. Networking is all about knowing people in your field, especially the influential or potentially influential ones, in order to strengthen your connections. The more connections you have, the wider your reach. The wider your reach, the better your chances of publicity and various opportunities. Remember?

In this chapter, we will get into the specifics about how to promote you and your brand.

First, we are going to revisit the idea that you are already an expert because of your experience. You already know your customers, their attitudes, and their needs as a result of engaging with the hospitality industry. We will explore how you can build upon that knowledge with your marketing.

Promotion has gone digital today, so our fundamental focus will be on social media. We are going to discuss promoting your brand content along with the trends of the Big Three social platforms – Facebook, Instagram, and LinkedIn. Following that, I have included a section on managing your social media profiles and finding potential new options, such as outreach programs and Email marketing.

Your Experience and Your Aspirations

If you think about it, there is a lot that could be seen as universal in the world of bartending and marketing. As a bartender behind the station, you are the most vigilant person in the bar, especially when the place is throbbing. You have to be mindful of your workplace with all its glassware, mixing equipment, and ingredients. You need to keep an eye on your customers, and keep track of their orders and checks, identify the regulars as well as the new customers among them. It is a laborious job that requires multi-tasking, and a master craftsperson to pull it off.

You are that skillful person and, as such, a natural for marketing. Marketers are also constantly managing multiple projects and campaigns at the same time. Dealing with various environments simultaneously is a critical part of the job. You juggle customer feedback, your employees, what's working and not working, your suppliers, and so on. In addition, as a marketer, you also keep track of your social media, emails, and engaging content. In the same way that you are in constant communication with your environment as a bartender, you are in constant communication with everyone involved in your business as a marketer.

All You Need to Know About Marketing You Already Learned Behind the Bar

Have you ever considered why and how people drink? They don't drink because they need alcohol or because only a particular brand of spirit will satisfy their desire. They drink to ease off from their harsh routines, to socialize, to take a chill pill, to fit in, and to escape their existential pains. For your customers, your brand and your drinks are merely a means to an end goal of solving their bigger issues of boredom and exhaustion.

Imagine if you would go into your customer's face promoting your brand, convincing them why they need your services. It would freak them out, and ruin the relationship you have. You can't do that. But what you can do, and have done as a bartender, is help make decisions for people who came to you already convinced that they need your drink. Why is that? Because people don't want to go to the trouble of deciding amongst options.

Customers very rarely approach you knowing exactly what they want. They ask YOU about what they should get. They either say, "What do you suggest I should get?" or "What's selling the most?" Now that's a key lesson to keep in mind when you start marketing. Your customers may not be swayed by your tricking them into believing they need a particular drink, but they will be sucked in by learning what's selling the most.

Companies and bartenders offer little deals (remember buybacks?) and as a result, engage people; this is how they win loyalty, and inspire customers to come back and spend more. This is the power of *mutual benefitting*. You can make them feel special, and consequently, you earn a special place in their hearts.

When the client asks for scotch on the rocks, you don't simply pour scotch on rocks and push the glass towards them. Instead, you pour the drink with an expert hand in style, whisking the ice so that it clinks against the glass. You make sure that the glass is pristine, and you gently pass it to them on a cocktail napkin, delivering your best Jay Gatsby smile.

As a marketer, you follow similar tactics – you *over-deliver*. Your communication and service actually make a bigger impact than the exceptionally good quality of your product. Your job as a marketer is not simply to get the word out about the product, but also to answer questions your users might have, and ensure their satisfaction. Make them feel like they are getting unique treatment. You can do this by creating a memorable experience for them. For instance, if you start a party bartending service, you make sure you give them the most joyous occasion you can possibly give them. Create a welcoming atmosphere and encourage your employees to get to know the customers through casual, yet unforced, conversation. Just like behind the bar. This happens at all stages and platforms of communication from email to social media, to smiling while you're on the phone. They can't see it, but they can sense you're smiling.

Networking

Once you master the basics of marketing, in both bartending and your business, you will come across as warm and friendly. Congratulations, you're networking. Chances are, you will get your regular chain of customers. Just like with bartending, the more your customers like your company as a brand, the more likely they will want to do business with you. Remember, we talked about incorporating your personality into your brand? Every transaction your customers have with your brand is their transaction with you. You are the image; your brand's reputation is your reputation. Remember that people are curious about your expertise. A question comes to mind. "How does that make me an expert?" One word: Visibility.

Which person's opinions do you think will hold more weight? Someone who has been bartending exceptionally well for a decade but has no social media profile? Or someone who may have just about half as much of experience and similar skills, but regularly posts on social media platforms to get their bar or brand's word out? The first

Jason Littrell

one may be great behind the bar (where she will stay) but will fade into obscurity and never be a brand. Our social media maven (the second choice) will headline industry events, get quoted in trade publications, and contribute expert opinions to articles, blog posts, broadcasts, and podcasts. If this is smarmy to you, you are going to have a hard time finding clients. This is how people establish themselves as experts, even if, in reality, they are not necessarily the smartest or even most knowledgeable individuals in the room. Ahem.

What Experts Have

Five Factors Associated with Expertise

Factor #1: Experts come highly recommended by friends and colleagues. In other words, they have a healthy network. (57%)

Factor #2: Experts are effective communicators with the ability to make complicated subjects easily understandable. They break it down so that a five-year-old could understand. (38%)

Factor #3: Experts are problem-solvers with a proven track record of success that's highly visible.

Experience, experience and more experience. (36%)

Factor #4: Experts inspire confidence when they speak. People stop in their tracks and listen to what they have to say. (31%)

Factor #5: Experts are published in prestigious publications – blogs, broadcasts, etc. (27%)

It is not difficult to establish yourself as an expert. I am pretty sure if you have been internalizing and operationalizing the information in this book, I would absolutely call you an expert. In truth, you always were, now you just have to sell yourself as one. This is where Social Media platforms come in.

Marketing with Social Media

It is important that you deliver your brand message on the right platform at the right times to the right audience. This is the essence of social media marketing. In this section, we will look at how to message your brand on Facebook, Instagram, and LinkedIn. It is also important to note that as a matter of course, all these social platforms are tracked by search engines. By engaging social media, you are lending relevance reach to your brand.

Facebook

When you think of Facebook, you think of chatting with friends, de-stressing by checking our pics and videos, and just relaxing. You can also join conversations and become part of a community. You probably don't associate very heavy content with Facebook. Other people don't either! So, if promoting (or advertising) on Facebook, you want your brand's message and content to come across as light-hearted and fun. You don't want to be seen as a business 'outsider' who tries to sell the brand aggressively. You could experiment with emojis (without overdoing it) and use other fun tools to give your brand a distinct feel.

Your Facebook business page: This is the site where you develop your brand identity while showing your human side. If you loosen up a bit, try not to be so serious, and slip in humor, you will end up with a brilliant place for your business and marketing. The sweet spot is a nice mix of humor, educational resources (believe it or not, you can add impressive statistics in a cool, light-hearted manner), and posts about updates. You want your clients to be talking about you everywhere.

Facebook Advertising: On the advertising side of things, you have Facebook ads, which appear on the side of your Facebook site or pop up on your phone or tablet screen. These classic ads are referred to more specifically as Marketplace Ads. They consist of a headline with a copy, an image, and a click-through link to either a Facebook page, a Facebook app, or another website. It is a good idea to reserve small but eloquently catchy chunks of your brand advertising for Facebook.

Sponsored Stories: The importance of Sponsored Stories cannot be overemphasized; they can be the most informal kind of advertisement that shows a user's interactions with your brand on your customer's feeds.

Sponsored Stories are the closest thing to word-of-mouth marketing as you will ever find on the Web. If a user sees that three of his friends like a certain page, he will be more inclined to pay attention. It follows the law of attraction; if your friends are buying it, you want to buy it. Encourage every customer to give you a shoutout on FB for a certain incentive or a giveaway.

Instagram

Compared to Facebook, Instagram posts tend to have a visual more authentic tone. Instagram algorithms are based on the user's interests, data about which it gleans from user searches and engagement.

Did you know that 80% of the Instagram user base is *outside* the U.S? This means it is the perfect platform to attract international customers and build a worldwide appeal. There are 25 million business profiles on Instagram. 80% of Instagram users follow at least one business, and 72% of users say they've purchased a product they've seen on the platform. This indicates that the app is highly preferred, not only for casual users, but for commercial uses too. Some Instagram-specific features to consider include:

Instagram Stories: The trend started with Snapchat, but many believe that Instagram has updated and taken stories to the next level. Features such as Instagram Live, and IGTV allow for a more multidimensional and creative experience for a customer to interact with their brand of choice.

Instagram Captions: Instagram captions are the Holy Grail of Web marketing. If you take the time to create articulate and appealing content that will delight and engage your customers, you will reap great rewards. With practice, you will get better at it. Good copy sells.

There are various things to consider with the captions, and one of the most important is the caption length. Users can only see the first two lines of each caption. What does that mean? That means the decision to read more is determined by your caption. To manage this, you can put the most important content at the beginning of the caption so that it is always visible.

But what if your first two lines are great, but the rest of your caption is incredibly long? Readers will simply move on. It is advisable to limit long captions to 100-150 words. This is not the law however. You may gradually rise to that stage, but for now, the rule is that brevity is the soul of Insta-appeal.

Linkedin

Your LinkedIn profile is the bossy-pants platform where you are wearing the suit and tie and very professionally selling yourself. You want to generate leads from clients, companies and followers, as well as build brand awareness and establish strategic partnerships. LinkedIn should be your go-to place for professional networking. You can connect your brand with hundreds of millions of professionals across the globe through this staggeringly vast social media platform (<u>and search engine</u>).

Personal Profile: Start with your own profile before starting with your brand. Think of yourself as the cover of a book; everybody will decide whether or not to read the book based on what they think of you. You will formally introduce yourself, your prospect, and your long-term goals and plans here. You will also mention your interests, your education and work experience--whatever is relevant. Through your personal LinkedIn profile, you will generate your identity in the business market. Use searchable keywords that describe your service multiple times.

Business Profile: On the other hand, your Company Page should offer ample opportunities for prospective customers to learn more about your company, the people who work there, and other business-related content. Your brand philosophy will be very much in evidence on this page.

It is always a good idea to connect your business profile with any staff you may have. Ask them to write and review their experience. Employees are your biggest advocates and are also the most likely to share your content with their networks. That will come to establish your brand's reputation outside the company.

Social Media Management (SMM)

After having reviewed different kinds of social media, you might be thinking, "This is the startup of my business; I am alone handling my business and my suppliers, and so on. On top of this, I have to manage all my social media platforms separately too?" The answer is, not exactly.

Social Media Management (SMM) software is like a hub that gives you centralized control over all your various profiles. When you're using these tools, you can connect various accounts, and you can manage all your social media and marketing from one place. This provides efficiency and convenience.

If you have SMM software, you get a lot done and automated from one dashboard. This means you will not have to switch to Facebook and use your business' Facebook voice to manage that particular style and then pulling all the way out and switching to your Instagram, and so on. SMM tools allow you to automate your posts and bulk-upload a bunch of Facebook or Instagram posts or put up a LinkedIn profile update. It allows you to conveniently *pre-plan everything*. All the important analytics also appear in one place. You easily keep track of your particular profile and how well it is doing. This is one of the best features that SMM tools allow.

My workflow: I use a SMM software called SocialBee because it allows me to chop up longer form content, and re-distribute it as evergreen content across all connected platforms. Every time I make a podcast, write a blog post, or make a video, it gets cut into smaller pieces with repurpose.io and re-distributed across all my channels as snippets of video content. The collective attention span is extremely short, so repurposing your long form content is the path to sanity and an automated workflow. I can say without any irony that if anything happened to me, and nobody turned off Socialbee, I would be tweeting and posting forever.

Hootsuite: Hootsuite is one of the most popular SMM softwares available. For $19 a month, you get the Professional program that offers to keep track of up to 10 social profiles. It integrates up to 160+ free and paid apps –Excel spreadsheets, for example – and allows you to save up to 350 posts across all profiles. You also get social analytics and reporting as part of this package.

Email Marketing: If you think that in this world of social media influence email is dead, you have another think coming. The truth is that email marketing is still going strong, and is possibly one of the best possible strategies for your business. Based on 2018 data, email marketing is still ranked as the most effective marketing channel, beating out social media, SEO (search engine optimization), and affiliate marketing.

However, there is an etiquette to making your way into people's inboxes. Getting into somebody's inbox is like getting invited to their home for dinner. If they ask you to take your shoes off, you respectfully do so. You have to ask people to allow you to send emails, but you can also do that in a catchy and creative manner.

You might think your email is special, but to the reader it might be SPAM (unwanted or unsolicited). This is especially true when your emails are universal for all your business contacts. To overcome this, you can move on to segmentation of your email lists after you have mastered the basics. Start sending separate types of emails to different groups of people and always work towards increased segmentation of the market.

In order to interest people in receiving emails and newsletters from you and your company – for announcing important updates you have been tirelessly working on – you have to establish your credibility. This is done by explaining what the emails are for when your user interacts with your product.

I deliver a weekly newsletter to my subscribers that drives traffic to my content from that week using an RSS feed. This drives traffic to my blog, YouTube channel, social media, and podcasts.

Online Presence in General

According to Google, 97% of consumers use the Web to search for local businesses. Having a strong online presence is an essential element of your marketing strategy, no matter what size your business is or what industry it belongs to.

It is vital to have an online presence for outbound marketing because it reinforces your brand and what you offer to your target market. Once you have communicated with your audience, you will need a Web presence that helps portray why your product or your service is so great.

An online presence is also vital for inbound marketing because quality online content will help attract the customers, even if they haven't heard of your brand. A business or a personal brand that maintains a Website is more likely to receive traffic by merely being there. According to Google and Nielsen, 73% of mobile searches trigger additional action and conversation, whereas 55% of purchase-related conversations take place within one hour of an initial mobile search.

When a new customer finds you on Google, when your engagement on your Facebook page is seen by others, when someone subscribes to your email list, or when someone finds you through online word of mouth, you know that you are doing something right. Maintaining an attractive online presence is worth the effort because it pays off in many measurable, attainable ways.

What Does It Mean to Have an Online Presence?

The term "online presence" means a lot of things. A few years ago, setting up your website meant that you had an online presence. It was enough to have a pleasant looking homepage, smart navigation, pretty image, and useful content. However, this is no longer true. There are so many other things involved in having an online presence today, such as:

- Website design and development
- Search engine optimization
- Blogging
- Social media marketing

Search Engine Optimization

For your website to rank higher on search engine results, it has to be optimized. Optimization involves the use of keywords that best describe your business, products, and services. These keywords are what your customers will type into a search engine to get the results they are looking for. For search engines to pick your website, it is crucial to optimize your pages, images, and content.

Should You Put a Blog on your Website?

Blogging is a great way to talk about what your business is doing and how you can help your existing and your potential customers. Blogging adds interactivity and authenticity to your website. Also, it encourages viewers to visit your site and stay on it longer. This is a key metric in SEO ranking. Blogging frequently and using good SEO will help you to appear on search engines more often. It might be necessary to do a certain amount of research about your blogging subjects. This does not involve weeks of research and frequent trips to the library. But, if you are going to post something to the public, you need to make sure that it is accurate and full of unique facts. This is not to say that your articles need to be 100% original, but this means that your readers will be looking for something new and educational to read.

For great keyword suggestions and blog topics that you can rank for, check out UBERSUGGEST.com and Answerthepublic.com

Ensuring Consistency on Your Website

You want to have a strong brand presence. Color is a way to differentiate and identify your products and services in a crowded marketplace. From the black and orange combination of the Amazon logo to the green of the Starbucks emblem, the shade you choose is a vital and most crucial element in brand recognition.

Given how color increases brand identification, it is important that the color remains consistent across all your branding media, whether online or in print. In the same way, quality use of color is essential. Imagine spending a hefty amount of money only to find out in the end that the color is poorly rendered and unrecognizable as yours. Keeping colors consist is difficult because:

- Every device is different.
- Every color copier is different.
- Every mobile screen is different.
- Every type of paper takes ink differently, depending on its weight and surface. It could be coated or uncoated paper.
- Engraving ink is different from offset ink.

- Short-run digital inks are different too; some are toner-based, whereas some are liquid ink.

To create consistency within your branding, you need to take the time to establish clear guidelines for the use of color in all of your online as well as print materials. Regularity in color goes a long way in promoting brand consistency, and this is key to making the brand memorable and enduring. This is known as a STYLE GUIDE.

Pick Your Keywords

This step starts with a simple list of keywords that match the services you are providing. When your list is complete, you can sign up for a free Google Adwords account. You do not have to create or fund an ad campaign. However, you will need the AdWords account to access the free Google Keyword Planner Tool. This tool lets you input your chosen keywords to find out how much traffic it can get. Also, it suggests any related keywords that you might have not even thought of.   What you're looking for here is terms people are ALREADY searching for. You want to capture that traffic by writing blog posts. If your blog posts are keyword optimized (e.g. several mentions, H1 tags, etc), they will rank higher in the search engines.

Setting up a Google My Business Presence

By creating a local page on Google My Business, your business information comes up in Google Search, Google Earth, and other Google properties. Think of your Google My Business page as a mini-Website that appears on Google Maps. It helps increase your overall online presence and provides a snapshot of your business. Also, it can give you a quick ranking boost.

Here's what you need to know:

- ✓ A personal Google account is needed to set-up a Google My Business account.
- ✓ Go to plus.google.com/pages/create and sign in to your Google account.
- ✓ Choose your business type:
- ✓ Storefront
- ✓ Service Area
- ✓ Brand
- ✓ Search for your business name. If your business does not appear, click on "Add your business."
- ✓ Enter in your business name, street address, city, state, zip, business phone, category, and click on "I deliver my goods and services to my customers:
- ✓ Click on "Continue."

- ✓ Choose the geographic radius where your business operates and click on "I also serve customers at my business address."
- ✓ Google will ask you to verify your info and agree to the terms of service.
- ✓ A Google+ page will automatically be created for your business. You will have to complete your business's profile as directed.
- ✓ Google needs all accounts to be verified with a code to set up. This code will be mailed to you via a postcard.
- ✓ Click on "Mail me my code" and add with it an optional contact name. Click on "Send a postcard." You should receive a postcard within 1-2 weeks. Once you receive the code, login to your Google+ dashboard at plus.google.com/u/0/dashboard. Choose your new page and enter the code to verify the My Business account. The code is only valid for 30 days.

This chapter was all about promoting and selling yourself. In the modern age, social media has become the biggest trend in marketing one's brand. That is why I have not even bothered to talk about direct mail, billboards, or TV advertising. If you are a startup, the big idea is that every time you create (or recreate) a piece of content, whether a cocktail or introduce a new menu, take a picture of it, and publish it along with an insightful story. Don't be afraid of giving away free content! You are not giving away your playbook; you're simply communicating that you know what you're doing. You are establishing yourself in the fast-changing world in a manner that the other bartenders aren't. That is not arrogance, that's confidence.

Chapter 9

Finding and Attracting Clients

*"There is only one boss, the customer —
and he can fire everybody in the company
from the chairman on down, simply by
spending his money somewhere else."*

Without customers, there is no business; nothing emphasizes that more strongly than this quote by Sam Walton. And no one knows that better than you, who deals with customers every day. Whether you want to become a brand ambassador, marketer, or an independent consultant, finding and keeping clients is the single biggest factor in determining whether your business will succeed or fail. **As a freelancer, your job is to get a job.**

Building your brand is a process that helps you discover and nail down new opportunities. The stronger your brand, the more customers you will attract, and the more leverage you will have in negotiating your fees and/or ownership percentage.

This chapter is about attracting clients. How do you find your customers, engage with them, and pull them toward you? Can you treat your competition with kindness and still present more opportunities for your customers and yourself? You will also learn that getting yourself exposure and learning how to hustle are essential to attracting new clients too.

The *Mise En Place* Approach to Client Acquisition

At this point, it is important to revise the concept of *mise en place* that we discussed at the beginning, which literally means "Put in Place" in French and is the cornerstone of the approaches we will take in this chapter.

The idea is that we need to prepare all the ingredients, tools, and components –but not the meals themselves - BEFORE the client orders something. This is so we can customize the customer's request efficiently, and ensure that the dish is ready and available when they need it. This is a concept you need to understand.

You have to similarly *"MISE"* your customer appeal.

Each client's requirement is specific according to their taste preferences and characters. You cannot have a restaurant with pre-prepared meals that performs optimally. You can, however, have all your tools ready so that when the order comes, you just add things together, cook them, and prepare them according to the demands of your clients.

What this means is that you have your homework done, you have done your research, you have your story down, and you know what your business is all about. When you finally approach the customer, your services are tailored just for them.

Your Client is Right in Front of You

Depending on what it is that you specialize in, EVERYONE is probably a potential client. It's important to understand that you ARE YOUR BRAND, and when you're out, you should always be "on." You never know which passer-by could be your next buyer,

which stranger on the train could be your
next client, which nice woman you meet at
a party could be your next loyal customer.
Therefore, you need to see and treat
everyone you meet as if they were
prospects because they are.

How I Got My First Consulting Job

It was just another day at the bar. I had just begun
to think about taking the plunge and branding
myself. I engaged and charmed a customer when I
was tending bar. It turns out that he was a bar
owner doing research on what his service offerings
were going to be. Through one conversation at a
slow bar during a shift, I managed to entice him to
hire me for a new bar consulting project—my first
one. The next day we negotiated. The next week I
had a deposit and was starting to implement
concepts for them.

Engaging the 'Guest'

Your client is your guest. They enter your
humble world, get a taste of your
hospitality, and hopefully take that
impression with them forever. If it is
pleasant, not only will they be eager to visit
again, but they will sing praises about your
hospitality to others too. If it is unpleasant,

then that's a missed opportunity likely never to be recovered.

You inspire your client just as you inspire your guest, who is in need of your service (whether they know it or not). You show them around the house, invite them to sit in the best and well-furnished place, serve them delicious meals, and then finally you talk shop. By that, I mean you share your brand's vision and what it offers for them.

Your goal is to paint a picture of their future in which your brand plays an important role. Make sure that the picture inspires them! I know this is hard, but this is essential and especially relevant for those of you who are just starting up.

Perfecting your Elevator Pitch

Sometimes, your guest is short of time and cannot stay for long. How do you explain to them what you do and have for them while being charming? In this case, you better make sure your story is short. This particular potential client or investor does not want your long story. This is where the elevator pitch comes in.

An Elevator Pitch is a description that sums up what you do or your business does so concisely that you can tell it during the average elevator ride. If you were to write it down, it would be less than 100 words. Here's what the listener needs to know:

- What is your product or service?
- Who is buying it?
- Who is your team?
- How do you make money?
- What is your value proposition?
- Who is behind the business?
- What is your vision? Where do you see yourself and your business?

Anyone reading this book is a potential competition. Do you think they're running through all these steps too? You bet. The elevator pitch is your first impression, and you must eloquently, confidently, and briefly communicate to your prospective client that you have the edge and what it takes to make them look like a star.

You need to ensure that you open your elevator pitch by drawing the listener's attention towards you through your passionate words and actions. Beware of sounding like you have memorized it, even if you have. They should, after their 60 seconds of attention, feel like the elevator ride was too short; they should get interested to hear more. If they are too busy, you could at least hand them your business card. DO NOT SELL AT THIS POINT. The intention is to get a meeting or a phone call to go into specifics.

Sample Elevator Pitch

> Hi! I'm <your name> from <your company> I work with <client description> to help people <concise summary of your immaculately crafted business description> servicing <client segment>. It's really fun working and serving my clients because of <your comparative advantage>. I also oversee <two descriptions/designations are better than one; mention a website/blog if you have one>. My goal is to <state business goal>. Here's my card if you want to learn more about our business and how we can help.

With the perfectly timed smile and inflexions, you will have their eyebrows raised. They are now looking at your business card, then putting it in their pocket and smiling back.

Play the numbers. If you deliver this pitch a thousand times, how many meetings do you think you'll get? If you get the meeting, you're much more likely to get the job.

Getting Involved in Trade Organizations

You are just one business operating within an industry, but you don't have to be the lone ranger. You have trade organizations that work like clubs for businesses within a particular industry. As a platform, trade organizations have many benefits for their members, which is why you should consider becoming one. Some of the advantages that trade organizations offer are:

Networking: Trade organizations are filled with potential contacts, clients, and partners who can help your business flourish, go to the next level, and be more noticeable in your industry. You attend its events, collaborate and socialize with the influential figures, get off-the-record tips, and generate possible shoutouts for your brand's social media.

Training and Education: Certifications and licenses that the trade organizations offer can be evidence and indicators of expertise, prestige, and reliability. Any outsider who does a profile on your brand and finds these accolades associated with it immediately perceives you as important (because you are). Through educational and developmental programs, you can learn about getting to the top of the industry, getting hands-on experience, and getting the exposure that leads to thought leadership and authority.

Influence: When you join an organization, the organization is not only doing you good; you are benefitting them too by aligning with the mission and philosophy of the association. A word of warning, this goes both ways.

Hustle: Your New Middle Name

Once you settle in with the motions of getting into the business, some doors will open up to you by themselves. Others, however, such as getting exposure and media attention, will only be gained if you fight tooth and nail. In this section, let's look at how the old-fashioned hustle attracts new customers and what the hustle looks like.

Become friends with your competitors: If you have stepped into the business, it is inevitable that you have done your research and know who your competition is. If you have done your homework well, you have learned a lot and even been inspired by these competitors. Gone are the days when the competition was thought of primarily as the enemy. In this age, good businesses, especially the ones that are up and coming, have different attitudes toward their competition. It is much better to be friends with your competition than enemies. Professional connections with brands that provide the same services as you, whether they are more successful than you or not, is an act of unity. Collaboration, when executed right, serves to elevate you and your competition in the business alike. It's not a "if you can't beat them, join them" attitude; it's more like "you help me and I help you."

Openness and friendliness towards your competition goes a long way. Animosity is short-lived and can be truly toxic. In the world of business where the majority of entrepreneurs are all about themselves, it becomes a virtue and something special to scroll and come across a picture of two owners with similar goals supporting each other's companies. This is the kind of business owner you want to be.

Get Press Coverage: No other type of exposure beats that of getting an article telling your story. Not so luckily for you, obtaining press coverage is not an easy job. It is a tough job, but is vital too, for it filters the tough entrepreneurs from the mediocre ones. It is a good prospect that requires tireless hustle and dedicated planning.

You are one step ahead of the competition already; you have set up your story. If your story is brilliant, half of your job is already done. If not, tweak it some more and have something in there that the media would love to portray. Something catchy, but not necessarily controversial. Just be someone with a captivating story, healthy social media, website, impressive logo and so on (which you should already have). Look at your brand through the eyes of a journalist and see that there should be no information that is inaccurate or missing. You should anticipate their questions and stockpile your answers and assets accordingly.

Mise the Journalist Connections:

That's right. We are back at it again. Just as you wouldn't ask a random train passenger to give you a shoutout on Instagram, it doesn't sound right to ask a journalist you do not know to write and publish on your brand either. You need to have journalist connections already in your pocket.

It is likely that you have never met a journalist let along become an acquaintance or a friend. The concept of *mise en place* still applies, for before you get the story entirely prepared, you need the resources. And you can get them through social media.

You can target your ideal journalists and follow them on social media. You don't have to aim straight for the national levels. A local or regional magazines or blogs would be a good start too.

Once you find appropriate journalists, flatter them, post their work and talk ridiculously about what you love about them. Chances are, you will get their attention, and they will be interested in you. If they don't approach you themselves, you can do it yourself after a time you think would be most appropriate. A good length of an investment would be two months. Remember, journalists are people too who are looking for work and stories.

A great resource for free press opportunities is called Help a Reporter Out (or HARO). This free email newsletter sends three times a day and is packed with requests from reporters looking for sources. Get on this list, and skim through and pitch yourself as an expert. It's that easy.

And Now A Word from the President

I second President of the United States Bartenders Guild (USBG), New York Chapter. The reason I campaigned for and got elected for the presidency was that I genuinely cared for its constituents. I also knew that in exchange for being at the end of the line for criticism, my name would get thrown around quite a bit. That was both a good thing and bad thing. As a volunteer, my compensation was notoriety plus an opportunity to learn how to organize a lot of people. This was a valuable stepping stone in my career, as I became a recognized brand, and got mentions in the local and national press.

This is one important reason that I was able to establish a healthy and lucrative customer inflow, while also serving my community as a volunteer.

I do recognize that engaging with people and becoming a member of organizations is demanding and draining. I know that not everyone is comfortable with the idea of selling themselves. I used to feel icky about telling friends that I wanted to pitch them on my business. Still, I wasn't just selling them something then walking away; I was offering a mutually beneficial partnership. If your service makes a person's life easier, you're doing a good thing. You become a magnet for clients.

Chapter 10

Business Planning and Growth

"....a great way to begin with the end in mind is to develop a personal mission statement, and to use that statement to guide all that you do."

– Stephen R. Covey

Planning your business doesn't require a business plan as much as it involves a business MODEL. Knowing where your business fits into the ecosystem of similar services allows you to nimbly operate in a world of competing interests. It's an anchor that keeps you grounded to your mission and essential intent.

I don't recommend sharing your business model with anyone who is not actively invested in your success. In fact, unless you're seeking outside investment, nobody really needs to see your plan.

Your business plan doesn't have to be a lengthy document with detailed financial projections and charts. It can be as simple as a one page document that outlines a few key elements of your business. Who you are, what you do, how you make money, and a brief description of your client and how you plan on approaching them.

This doesn't have to be a tattoo either. This can change with the times, tides, and trends. Be sure not to get too stuck on this. Maybe spend an hour building yours. Your plan is a consolidation of all the elements we have discussed in this book. I keep mine in a desk drawer for review periodically to make sure I'm staying on track, on brand, and on mission.

The Side Hustle...

A common misconception about starting a businesses is that you need to start with a bang. It requires a lot of your time, requires you to quit your job, and kiss your family good-bye for awhile. It doesn't have to be this way. Many business owners start their businesses as side ventures.

They do not have to quit their jobs. Instead, they can use their skills to start a business on the side. They do not have high expectations that their businesses will pay the bills, but they do not limit themselves to growth either. Here are some rules to consider when starting part time:

The Business Plan: Start with the End in Mind

What does it mean to "begin with the end in mind?" In business, you always need a plan. Without a properly written plan, you will face trials and errors. Simply put, you will be executing tactics without a properly framed strategy.

The plan is the foundation for goal setting. You need to identify and measure successes. Along the way, you will need to revise your goals, strategies, and plans depending on the trending needs and challenges of your customers.

According to Stephen Covey, everything has to be created twice. First is the initial blueprints, and then comes the physical production. Before considering the blueprint, you need to understand the values of your business. After you have set your goals, create a mission statement.

Your mission statement should state what is essential to your business, what you are aiming to achieve, and how do you propose to do it. Your mission statement is a combination of the vision of the business and the mission. It focuses on the values of your organization and sets the highest goal reachable.

After crafting your mission statement, you will review and revise it as much as you can. Every goal in your plan needs to meet the goals of the organization. If you feel that a task does not bring you closer to achieving those goals, you can always revise it or even discard it. The key is to stay focused and aware of what is going on in your business. You need to make sure that you accomplish your short-term goals that contribute to the bigger picture.

It may seem off, but the best place to begin with is at the finish line. Similarly, it is easier to climb down the mountain than trekking upwards. Therefore, imagine your ultimate business goal. What is your be-all and end-all for your business? Instead of stabbing blindly towards possible successes, decide on which success you are headed for. And then create a plan to make that goal a reality.

Innovation: The Key to Growing Your Business

Coming up with new ideas is crucial for a business. With new ideas, a business is able to improve its process, bring new products and services to the market, increase efficiency, and improve profits. Marketplaces are becoming more competitive with each day. Competition has increased, which leads to broader access to technologies. This has further led to an increase in trading and extensive knowledge sharing across borders.

Innovation can be a single breakthrough-- a new product or service. Or it can also be a series of small upgraded changes. Whatever form it takes, innovation is a process of creation. Innovative ideas come from either inside the business (employees, managers, or in-house R&D) or from outside the business (suppliers, customers, market researches, media reports).

Introducing innovation can help in improving productivity, reducing costs, being more competitive, building the value of your brand, establishing new relationships, increasing turnover, and improving profitability.

Businesses that fail to innovate run the risk of losing the market share to competitors, deteriorating productivity, losing staff, experiencing reduced margins and profits, or even the risk of going out of business.

There are many sources that you can use that will help in generating new ideas for your business. Everyone involved in your business (suppliers, business partners, and business contacts) can contribute ideas to your business process as well as provide support and encouragement. When running your business, you need to provide equal opportunities to everyone to add in their ideas for innovation.

Promoting Innovation

To promote innovation in your business, you need to:

- Make sure that you have the proper processes and events to capture ideas.
- Create a community for people to gather and brainstorm ideas.
- Create an atmosphere for people to express their ideas without having to face any criticism.
- Encourage taking risks. Do not penalize people who fail in their new ideas.
- Promote an environment of openness between individuals and teams. Good ideas should be shared with others. Teamwork

should be promoted to help in sharing ideas and information with everyone.

- Focus on the fact that people of all levels of the business share responsibility for innovation. Therefore everybody feels responsible for taking the business forward.
- Give rewards for innovation and success. Incentive plays a significant role in encouraging staff to think creatively.
- Look for imagination and creative traits when recruiting employees.

Partnerships

Great partnerships originate from great businesses. However, even great businesses can fail due to bad alliances. A partnership in a business is almost the same as a personal partnership. Both business and personal partnership involve:

- Investing in a common purpose
- Sharing skills and resources
- Sharing the profits and the loss

A business partnership is a legal relationship that is formed by two or more individuals to run a business as co-owners. The partners invest in the business and share its profits and losses.

Some partnerships are structured so that one individual works for the business, and the other might have limited participation in the business. It all depends on the agreement that all partners have.

Types of Partners in a Partnership

A partnership has different kinds of partners, depending on the type of partnership and the levels of partnerships.

- General partners take part in managing the partnership and have liability for debts of the partnership.
- Limited partners invest but do not participate in the management.
- Equity partners are those who only have a share in ownership.
- Salaried partners are the ones who are paid as employees.
- Different levels of partners, like junior and senior partners, may have various duties, responsibilities, and levels of input and investments.

Partnerships are registered with the state where the business is operating. However, the requirements of the registration and the types of partnerships vary from state to state. Partnerships use an agreement called the partnership agreement to clarify the level of the relationship between partners, their responsibilities, and their shares in the profits and losses of the partnership. This partnership agreement is limited to the partners and is not registered with the state.

Criteria to Consider Before Partnering Up

#1: Trust Your Gut but Write Everything Down: One of the biggest mistakes in a partnership is not clarifying each other's roles, compensations, responsibilities, boundaries, exit strategies, and getting these terms in writing. Yes, it is important to trust each other. However, it is also essential to make sure that you and your partner are on the same page before you begin your business venture together. People have their own sense of understanding. It is always a safe option to write down everything with a lawyer.

#2: Know Your Partner for At Least a Year: Before getting into a business partnership, it is best to get to know someone for at least a year. A business partnership is like a marriage, and before marriage, you need some time to just date for a while. Also, you need some time to get to know your partner, gather some references, and then

decide. If it doesn't work out, you move on. It is almost like choosing not to date the person after the third date. You haven't made any commitments, and you can amicably go your separate ways.

#3: Look for Someone Better Than You: You should look for a partner who is better than you in certain things. There have been instances where people's egos prevent them from having great partnerships. Above all, you need to make sure that you are going to enjoy your journey as partners. This business and your partner are going to be a big part of your life. There will be a lot of turmoil. Be wise enough to pick a partner who can weather the ups and downs with you, and who also might be fun to have a beer with along the way.

#4: Be Honest When Assessing a Potential Partner. It is essential to know the personality type of your potential partner. Try to understand their thoughts and personality traits. It is also essential to look for people who have different, complementary skills to your own and, most importantly, who share the same vision as you do. It is not enough to like someone to build a partnership with them. You will need somebody who is everything that you are not.

#5: Get on the Same Page: Form partnerships that are a win-win and are long term. Create a

contract that documents your understandings if ever the leadership changes. Sit with your partner to discuss core values and future business goals. You should check for alignments and allow both parties to develop trust by understanding each other's motives. Also, outline your expectations and commitments in your partnership so that they are addressed when planning. Together, this creates a healthy, profitable partnership that can withstand the stresses of business.

#6: Communicate. Make sure that you and your partner's goals are aligned. Do not be afraid to confront each other and talk openly with each other about any problems facing the business. Delaying the decision to end a partnership will do nothing more than create a lot of unnecessary issues and waste the energy that you should have used for something useful.

Having taken on a partner in the past, I learned a lot of these lessons the hard way, and I still feel the ripple effects of it. Do not take on a partner lightly. Make sure there is a clear path to the value they will receive and create, and STAY IN YOUR LANE. The reason my partnership didn't work out and we got 'divorced' was because I did not clearly communicate my expectations, and we did not clearly define what 'done' looked like. Additionally, we did not discuss each other's specific responsibilities.

Another parting piece of advice on this topic is to clearly outline the hierarchy and voting rules. If you're bringing a partner IN, you must retain control of your company.

PART 3: YOU

Chapter 11

Failure

"Success consists of going from failure to failure without loss of enthusiasm."

– Winston Churchill

No one likes to fail. No one works hard to fail. Failure does not feel good. It costs a lot of money and time, and sometimes strips you of your dignity. However, failure is an inevitable part of life. It is unavoidable and completely okay. As a matter of fact, sometimes, it is necessary to fail. Failure makes us more interesting. Learning how to fail and then get back up is a valuable skill. You need to have that this tenacity in order to succeed.

Let my experience be an example for you to get the idea. I was working on a job, producing cocktails for a new cocktail festival in Oregon. I was not prepared to produce this amount of complex drinks for such a big event and I failed miserably and publicly. This was one of the most humbling points of my career. Notwithstanding the fact that there was no one else to blame, I took full responsibility and swallowed the shameful embarrassment of failure. The clients were understandably upset. I groveled. We worked together to improve the quality of the program, and I was able to salvage my relationship with them.

Swallowing my pride and accepting my failure made things go smoothly for me, not only in the short run, but also in the long run.

Research shows that when fear of failure is paired with the feelings of incompetence, it can lead to a kind of procrastination and even paralysis that is self-sabotaging. So, if you are afraid of failure and do not believe in yourself, then you are going to fail because our ancient lizard brain will insist on it. On the other hand, if you are afraid to fail but consider yourself capable of achieving your goals, you are definitely going to succeed…eventually.

Why Is Failure Good for Success?

The sweetest victory is the one that is the most difficult. Achieving great success requires you to reach deep inside, fight with everything you have, and be willing to leave everything out there on the battlefield without knowing if your effort is enough or not.

Failure is often an important stepping stone to later success. This was the case with Thomas Edison, who invented the light bulb. It took him 1,000 tries before he developed a successful prototype. According to him, the light bulb was "an invention with 1,000 steps."

Unlike Edison, we try to avoid failure. As a matter of fact, we are so focused on not failing that we do not aim for success and we settle for a life of mediocrity. When we make mistakes and take the wrong steps, we gloss over and edit out the mistakes in our life. People see success as positive and failure as negative. But Edison's quote shows us that failure is not entirely a bad thing. You can learn, grow, and evolve from your past mistakes. You can look at your failures as steps toward success.

In business, failure is exceedingly common; nine out of 10 small businesses fail. The statistic may shock you but is necessary to know. Failing once, twice, or even a hundred times does not mean that you have reached the end of the road. It simply means that you have taken another turn and now you are one step closer to success. As you go through life and encounter failures, you will learn valuable lessons from those mistakes. Few entrepreneurs will tell you that their current successful business was their very first attempt.

How to Learn from Failure

Rule #1: Stay Humble: When you are doing well in life, you may feel invincible and like nothing can stop you; you are on top of the world. However, when you fail, it hurts. Sometimes, it hurts so badly that you feel like you will never be successful again. Staying humble helps improve the feeling of loss and failure. When you are drunk on success, you should never forget that you are human. You should treat everyone with the same humility and respect that you expect in return. When you are humble, you are mentally prepared for failure when it comes for you. And it will come for you.

Rule #2: Learn from Your Mistakes: It is impossible to find a story of success that does not have a trail of mistakes behind it. Everyone experiences failure at one point or another in life.

The key to overcoming obstacles and becoming successful starts with learning from your mistakes. When you come across failure, you need to ask yourself why it happened. Was it because of something you did? Or did an outside force that played a part? You should not be afraid to be accountable for failure. In a lot of cases, something could have been done differently to prevent the collapse. It is your job to think deeply about your situation and not be afraid to do a little soul-searching.

Rule #3: Embrace Change: One of the best ways to learn from your failures is by embracing change. Some people hate change, and it is easy to understand why. People get caught up in their ways. They are used to seeing the same people at work and are okay with the routine. But you're not like that. When you fail, you might have to make drastic changes. If things are not going as you expected, you have to start over. Sometimes, you may have to sit back and look at the changes you need to make and embrace them. If you are looking to become a healthy entrepreneur, you have to be mentally healthy, which means that sooner or later you are going to experience failure. That's change, but it's good for you.

Rule #4: Filter Your Ideas: There is a saying that for every good idea, there are 100 bad ones. That means you need at least 100 ideas in order to get one good idea. When you are on a roll, it is easy to get tempted to act on every business idea that comes to mind. Slow down! Take notes, and review them from time to time. You can carry around a small notepad or download an app on your phone (I use workflowy). You will quickly see that not every idea that comes to mind is going to work.

You need to take the time to organize your thoughts after a failure and realize what you did wrong. Above all, you need to have the will to learn and grow. Anyone can succeed, it all comes down to how badly you want it. There is no success without failure. As you pursue your dreams, know that you are going to fail. There is a famous saying that failure does not stop people; it is how people handle failure that stops them. When you encounter failure, you need to tackle it head-on and learn from your mistakes.

The Benefits of Failure

Some people have huge misconceptions about failure. You may have even heard some people say that failure defines us. This could not be further from the truth. Failure is actually a good thing and we need a healthy dose of it from time to time. Here are six reasons why failure is good:

Reason #1: Failure Functions as a Reality Check: Sometimes, failing at something, even if you desire it truly, indicates that something is wrong somewhere. Use the lesson to see and evaluate what is going on with your situation and why things didn't work.

Reason #2: The Lessons Learned from Failure Are Priceless: Failure gives us an opportunity to learn from mistaken actions and do what is right the next time thus increasing your value in experience. Depending on how you look at it, I bill higher because of my failures.

Reason #3: This Is Not a World of 'One Shot Only': We live in a prosperous country that typically offers more than one opportunity to do anything. There are always second chances and, in some cases, even 100. If you fail once, try again to make things better. By all means, however, don't make the same mistake again. All you have to do is not be too blinded by the hurt of your previous failure to see them.

Reason #4: Failure Builds Character: Anyone can be the hero when times are good. But how do you measure up when the going gets tough? Do you crumble like a sandcastle, or stand your ground and keep smiling while focusing on where you want to be? Going through failure is actually a remarkable test of your character, courage, determination, and mindset. Failure is a kind of benchmark that will show you what you are made of.

Reason #5: Failure Drives You: You can use failure to your advantage. Use failure as a tool to strengthen your determination.

Reason #6: Everybody Fails: If you think those who achieved success were lucky, or the success was handed to them on a plate, you are probably wrong. People like Steven Spielberg, Steve Jobs, and Sylvester Stallone are examples of how failure led them to success in the long run.

Failure is Good for Business

If you are not failing, you are not winning either. You're not trying hard enough. If everything you do is working, it means you are not taking enough risks. This means, even if you are achieving small wins every day, you are not challenging yourself to achieve big wins that will set you apart from the rest. By taking risks and accepting that it is possible to fail, you can achieve what you have been working for. Your life and career are made up of many small but innately important choices. These choices may be right or wrong.

We all know that we do not know everything; this is why we seek new perspectives that challenge our assumptions. We are also aware that we will eventually make better decisions for the business when everyone is given the opportunity to bring their unique perspectives to the table. Rapid growth is not possible if you are not learning constantly, testing constantly what you think may work, and then iterating based on what you discover.

When someone on your team fails, celebrate it and talk about it. Embrace it and learn from it; make this the center of your business culture. With this practice, it becomes easier and easier to publicly share what actually went wrong and what the team can learn from that failure for the next time.

Honest, Shared Failure is Okay

Building your brand successfully does not hinge on avoiding failure. After all, countless leaders such as Walt Disney, Bill Gates, and Steve Jobs failed long before they succeeded. Your brand can transcend failure if you choose to take charge of it and persevere. As much as we value great stories of overcoming failure, people do not always hear them. When reading a resume, we focus on the triumphs and accomplishments and not the setbacks. Failures are often invisible whereas the successes are visible. This is why others get the impression that most things work out for successful people.

Many of today's leaders realize the importance of honest, shared understanding of their successes and failures. Let's take the example of hedge fund entrepreneur and Bridgewater founder, Ray Dalio. He gave a TED talk discussing an email that he had received from a junior employee blasting him for his poor performance at a meeting. The email read that Dalio deserved a *D* for his performance. It read that he had not prepared at all because there was no way he could have been that disorganized. He responded with an apology saying, "I'm sorry I let you down."

Being the boss, Dalio could have easily buried this criticism and lashed out against the source. But, instead, he owned his mistake and found a way to strengthen his brand through accountability and openness to feedback and encouraging others to give feedback like that in the future.

It is a natural instinct to want to hear good things about yourself, enjoy your successes, and hope that a conversation with your mentor is a lengthy list of praises. However, the reality is that failure is inevitable. With any business, failures, whether big or small, are bound to follow. So, when you stand face to face with a failure, it all comes down to how you handle it and how you let it impact your brand.

Don't Give Up

Passion is a strong liking or desire for some activity, object, or concept. But passion is more than just a strong liking; it is love multiplied by determination.

It is the kind of love or infatuation that sets a fire in your gut. It is the incredible yearning for something that is so amazing that you cannot imagine your life without it.

Some people don't really know what their passion is. They spend their lives unaware of what sparks their drive. Some even spend their lives living in a state of *whatever*. These people go through life, completing tasks and doing activities that seem normal to them. If you are lucky enough to find your passion, then you need to stick with it. Everything happens for a reason and your passion is there for a reason.

When working to achieve your passion, it is not difficult to become overwhelmed. There may be times when you want to give up on your goals, but you should never give up on a goal that is very important to you. Here are the reasons why you should never give up.

Reason #1: Life is not about talk, it is all about commitment: A dream is not worth anything until you put it into practice. When you dedicate yourself to achieving your dream, you find yourself at the intersection of perception and reality. You may have had the idea for years in your mind and it must be taking on a particular shape existing as a function of your imagination. When you put it to the test, it is time to get real. It is time to give birth to the idea and commit to nurturing it the same way you nurture a child.

Reason #2: Resilience and adaptation are the keys to vibrant life and healthy mind:
When you are working to manifest an idea, there will be setbacks, failures, and disappointments. They are good for you. They are the best teachers. Giving up is like dropping out of school. You end up missing out on critical experiences, important lessons, and not learning the enormous value of failure.

Reason #3: Quitting becomes a habit: If you give up on the things that matter the most to you, you will establish a pattern of giving up when things don't go the way you hope them to. You will not be able to learn the importance of persistence. Remember, anything worthwhile requires persistence.

Reason #4: Values are the most important:
Persisting toward achieving goals that are important to you means placing the most

significance on your values instead of your convenience. Hopefully, you wouldn't give up on your values and on the ideas that reflect those values.

Reason #5: Self-belief is everything: Giving up on your goals is like giving up on yourself. You are a unique person with your own gifts and talents. No one will ever invest in you more than you do. Millions of people may have had the same goals and dreams as you, but everyone manifests these dreams differently. Never giving up means to believe in yourself. It means to have the willingness to accept *failure* so you can learn the skill of adaptation. It means not to compromise on your most important values and walking the walk instead of just talking the talk. It means to live the life you want and are passionate about.

Consistent Effort Has Everything to Do with Your Success

A huge part of success is putting the time and effort in each day. Nobody does great things without work. Hard work is the baseline of great achievements. Nothing spectacular comes without it. Getting organized is hard work. Setting goals and planning to achieve them and staying on track is hard work. People do not fail to succeed. They fail to make an effort to succeed. To succeed in any industry of your choice, you need to make a commitment to put in all your efforts.

Greatness is not handed to anyone. The best people in the field are those who devote most of their hours to refining their craft. All the successful people mentioned in this chapter have failed and have worked hard to make it in life. You may rise slowly, but you are sure to rise. Forward is the only direction. Speed is immaterial.

There are no short cuts to lasting success. Many people do what is easiest, only to avoid hard work, and that is why you should do the opposite. Lasting success can only be achieved if you put in the sustained effort. It takes time, patience, and lots of hard work to see your way to the top in any business.

Time and energy are precious because they are very limited. In life, you can either be the hammer or the nail. You can apply force and energy wherever you want it to go, or you can react to the force and energy of others. To succeed, you have to decide what to do, where it fits in your day and how to get it done.

Chapter 12

Self-Care

"Self-care is never a selfish act—it is simply good stewardship of the only gift I have, the gift I was put on earth to offer to others."
--Parker Palmer

Working eighteen hours a day, seven days a week, is not sustainable. Your customers want YOU, regardless of the name of your business, the branding, logo design, etc. Taking care of yourself and ensuring your ability to produce the best products and services for your customers will improve not only the longevity of your career but also your life.

I used to attend all the industry parties around town, and I drank at all of them. Not just samples or testers, but the whole thing, and went back for second rounds. Be sure to present a professional image and listen to people. Seek to understand before seeking to be understood. Only then will your customers clamor for you.

When you have your own business, it is common to expect to be available 24 hours a day and seven days a week. Yes, business owners end up eating their lunch on their desks sometimes, but how many meals are you missing with your family? People talk about living a life of balance, but how do you do that when work is draining your energy? How do you replace that energy?

With a lot of neglected aspects of your life competing for the little time you have left after work, regular exercise loses its appeal. Long exhausting hours leave you feeling too tired even to prepare nutritious meals. And instead, quicker fixes like fast food and snacks become much more appealing. This is an easy habit to fall into.

The work-hard culture goes hand-in-hand with a play-hard culture. After a tough day at work, drinking becomes a welcome release. However, drinking regularly increases your chances of developing conditions like anemia, cancer, cardiovascular disease, cirrhosis, dementia, and depression. We feel like we're immune to these conditions when we're young.

How to Balance your Professional and Personal life

When we talk about work-life balance, we are talking about allowing yourself quality time in professional and personal spheres of your life. Being deeply engrossed in one area of your life means that you are neglecting the other one, which is also essential. If you are caught up in one specific area of your life, you may not feel calm or clear-headed or even motivated. You may feel as if your life is out of control.

So how do we get out of this downward spiral? Maintaining work-life balance involves giving time to all elements in life, both internal or external. Internal elements include your mind, your spirit, your physical health, and your spiritual health.

There are many techniques that you can use to maintain a work-life balance in your life. However, the simplest way to introduce the balance in your life is to adhere to the following steps:

- Be aware of everything that you are doing and not doing.
- "No" is a complete sentence. If you want to say 'no' to something, say 'no' without feeling as though you have to explain yourself.
- Identify your dreams and aspirations. If you don't, who will?
- Create your own goals. If you don't set personal goals, who will set them for you?
- Identify and embrace change. It is easy to say that you want to have a balanced life, but if you don't identify and embrace the changes you have to make, will you be able to?
- Set your priorities.
- Evaluate your decisions. Sometimes decisions are made by focusing on what other people want or require. This may be the right thing to do, but only when you have evaluated the decision.
- Trust your gut feeling. If your inner being feels that you want to do something or not do something, then you need to follow your intuition.
- Plan your time and include time for you even if you have to schedule it.
- Be level-headed. It is easy to impact your own time and balance of life when something challenging or negative happens.

You have to deal with these in a timely, thoughtful, and understanding way.

- Nurture yourself and make sure that you are allowing time for you as you focus on the time required for everything else.
- Listen to your body because it is your body that will tell you if you are not eating well or not exercising regularly. And if you do not listen to it and fall ill, you are impacting your life balance.
- Don't try to be all things to all people. You just have to be you. That's enough.
- Find the support circle like a coach, a mentor, like-minded friends, and more. You do not have to do everything yourself, you have to find support, and with a motivating support circle, you will be able to create your own balanced life.

Importance of Having a Daily Routine

Poor mental health is disruptive. Not having a steady daily routine leaves us feeling out of balance. Often, we have to make adjustments in our lives so we can make room for recovery. It may sound counter-intuitive, but developing a daily routine can help with maintaining mental health which in turn allows for better adaptation and available headspace in your business. It can help in coping with change, form healthy habits, and reduce stress levels.

In my experience, it wasn't until much later in my career that I began to value routines for my physical and mental health. It has been years now that I practice a daily routine of fasting, stretching, meditation, and physical exercise that powers me through my days. The way you take care of yourself is totally personal. Don't ever let anyone tell you what you should and shouldn't do, but at least consider everything. Here are some reasons for routines...

Reason #1: Routine Anchors Us: A routine can be an anchor. No matter what goes on in our day, knowing that having dinner around 6 pm, and going to bed around 10 pm, is a real comfort. The certainty of a routine can help manage the uncertainty that life often throws at you.

Reason #2: Routine Reduces Stress: Having a daily routine will help reduce your stress levels. Trying to remember things can be stressful, and can fill our brains up with everything on the 'to-do' list. When you have a routine, a lot of the things you do fall into slots, and you don't have to remember doing them anymore. For example, when you are well, you don't have to remember to brush your teeth because you already know by habit that teeth-cleaning comes after breakfast every day. Routine can take the guesswork and uncertainty out of our day. This allows us to feel more in control, and less decisions have to be made.

Reason #3: Routine Builds Daily Healthy Habits: Having a routine helps cultivate positive daily habits and prioritize self-care. Organizing your time allows you to build in blocks of time for things that are important to you. This will enable you to develop daily habits that help you with your mental health, like taking out time to relax and reading a book before bedtime. When things become a part of your routine, it becomes easier to keep up with them because we have the time to do them, and they become your "new normal."

Reason #4: Routine Improves Your Sleep: Sleep is essential for our mental health because going to bed and waking up at a fixed time allows our body to get used to the sleep-wake cycle and sets our sleep-wake clock accordingly. This means that by having a regular sleep routine, you will find it is easier to get sleep and sleep better once you are asleep.

Reason #5: Routine Builds Time for Important Things: Creating a routine allows you to build time for the important things. This includes time to rest, relax, and have fun. There are always going to be days when something out of the ordinary would happen, like a day at the job would take three times as long as you thought it would take, or someone might pop in unexpectedly and ask you to spend time with them. But structuring your time to include some downtime increases the likelihood that you will manage uncertainties in life really well. We all value different things, and that is why your daily routines are individual to you.

Reason #6: Routine Encourages Healthy Diet:
There are times when you are going through a rough patch and struggling to take a break. In that stage, it becomes tough to plan, cook, and eat a balanced diet. Food plays an essential role in our lives. It affects our mood. Therefore, we must try to keep things as balanced as possible. A routine is what can help with this because it allows us to spare some time for cooking, eating, and cleaning up afterward.

Reason #7: Routine Makes It Easier to Exercise:
Incorporating exercise into your routine is also essential. Not all of us are fans of exercising, but exercising can boost your mental calm. The main barrier to regular exercise is time. It can be challenging to fit exercise in your daily routine, especially when life gets busy. But even if you exercise only a couple of times a week and make time to indulge in an exercise of your choice, it would suffice. I do the hardest things first.

My daily routine is my anchor. It's my rock. But it actually starts at about 8pm each night. My routine is very personal because my life is different from your life.

My Daily Routine

- 8pm alarm - This lets me know it's time to start planning the day tomorrow. This is when I pick up the house, fold the laundry, tidy up, and eliminate or reduce any barriers to my success the next day. While I'm picking up, I think about the three most important things I want to accomplish the next day and put them in my to-do list as a priority.
- 9pm alarm – This means no more screens unless we'd planned to watch a movie or a show. This time is for reading, and learning. Taking my eyes off a screen also helps me get in to resting mode, and improves my sleep.
- 10pm – Bedtime.
- 5am – Wake up and work out. I like to get this out of the way first thing because it lends to mental clarity, and gives me a boost of endorphins to make me feel good and start the day on a positive note. In this time I also mediatate and do a breathing exercise called the Wim Hof Method. After all this comes the cold shower. Yep, it's

awesome. Try it. I'll read until my kid wakes up if there's extra time.

- 7am – Kid wakes up. I make breakfast, and we play until it's time to go to work.
- 9am – Work time! This is when my time blocking comes in to play. I block off my week in to sections including CEO work, focus work, client work, content creation, and Family time. I make sure I allot a certain amount of time for each of these elements so each one gets fair attention. Absolutely nothing work related happens on the weekends. That time is sacred.
- 5pm – Family time. We eat dinner together most days.
- 7pm – Put the kid to bed and do low priority work tasks from my phone if I feel like it.

It may seem very rigid, but this system allows me to get everything that needs to get done accomplished in a week. I keep track of my work product in Trello and I can see exactly what I've accomplished. There will not always be more time, but there will always be more work. So I just let it go.

Chapter 13

Final Thoughts

This book has provided you with a step-by-step guide on how to steer the wheel of your career on your own terms. It is about stepping up, negotiating, and planning for a better future for yourself and your family.

Starting your own business is not a challenge, but running it is. Yes, you will be taking some risks to start your business, but sustaining it is the real game. How is this different from shift work?

You need to believe in your brand. You need to understand that no one can be a master of everything. You may not be capable of painting a masterpiece or a perfect business plan, but that does not really matter. If you are intrigued and motivated to start a business, you already have all the tools you need.

You already have all the skills that will determine your value as a business owner. You do not have to compare yourself with others. And if you think that you do not possess any talents or skills, you need to look closer. You will eventually come up with something unique and different from the rest. When you find the unique expertise that you possess, you can go on to capitalize on these skills to establish your own brand.

Gathering information on how to run a successful bar does not mean that you browse through libraries or attend different workshops. You can take inspiration from other entrepreneurs and business owners and decide what works best for you.

As a bartender, multitasking is second nature. You have your attention on the glassware, the mixing equipment, and the ingredients you are adding to the drink. Also, you have your eyes on the customers. As a bartender, your job is to help people decide what they need. People dread the idea of deciding among a great list of choices. Your intervention here is the essence of marketing. Apply to this business.

Despite all the hard work you do, you may reach a point where you are about to give up, thinking that you are not as successful as you should be. But you need to keep in mind that success is built on a mountain of mistakes. Achieving success takes a long time. The longer you work for success, the more you learn from your mistakes and your failures. This leads to you becoming an expert in what you do.

It is your failure that actually makes you succeed. People today try their best not to fail. In fact, they fear failure. With the fear of failure, people eventually settle for mediocrity. Making wrong decisions allows you to improve and not make the same mistakes in the future. You learn, grow, and evolve from your mistakes.

It is my sincere hope that you gained a thorough and detailed perspective on how I built my business stemming from my skills and experience as a bartender. It has been my pleasure to share it with you, and I hope that you would pass it on to your team, and peers. This isn't the easiest path, but it is the self-directed one.

Thank you.

Acknowledgments

In this book I talk a lot about mentorship and working with a team. This book would not have been possible without the relentless support of the following people.

It takes a lot out of you to write a book, and you sometimes find yourself looking at a blank page with an empty cursor. The frustration that arises out of this emotional labor often comes at the expense of one's family in the form of shortness, tiredness, and quiet exasperation. To my wife, Brittany, thank you for your patience and limitless support.

xx

This book was edited by my Mom, Jan Littrell, and her insight from being a lifelong student was the single biggest factor in getting this done. She was a phenomenal cheerleader, coach, and ruthless editor and for that (and for changing my diapers), thank you.

To my family, you have always been the foundation on which all my successes (and numerous) failures have been built. Thank you for always beliving in my hairbrained schemes. Missy, Johnny, Dad, Charlie, Uncle Jimmy, Andrea, Corey, Matt, Uncle Wooj, Aunt Bonnie, and all of your crazy pets and children.

To the people mentioned in this book, thank you for providing inspiration to write about. Your accomplishments were uplifting and I am proud to use you as examples to aspire to.

To my former bosses. Thank you for giving me the chance to work for you. Because of the opportunities you created, I build a career, and a life I love. Hari Kalyan, Dave Plate, Dave Kaplan, Alex Day and to everyone else who had fired me over the years.

Lastly, I would like to thank you for supporting this idea and reading this far. It's your open minds and hearts that allowed this information in, and I truly hope you found its contents meaningful and worthy of your time to read it. Thank you.

Jason Littrell

www.ingramcontent.com/pod-product-compliance
Lightning Source LLC
Chambersburg PA
CBHW070925210326
41520CB00021B/6802